Studies in the

Drar

Henry Edward Krehbiel

Alpha Editions

This edition published in 2024

ISBN : 9789364737425

Design and Setting By
Alpha Editions
www.alphaedis.com
Email - info@alphaedis.com

As per information held with us this book is in Public Domain.
This book is a reproduction of an important historical work. Alpha Editions uses the best technology to reproduce historical work in the same manner it was first published to preserve its original nature. Any marks or number seen are left intentionally to preserve its true form.

Contents

CHAPTER I. THE WAGNERIAN DRAMA: ITS PROTOTYPES AND ELEMENTS...- 1 -

CHAPTER II. "TRISTAN UND ISOLDE."..............................- 22 -

CHAPTER III. "DIE MEISTERSINGER VON NÜRNBERG." ....- 42 -

CHAPTER IV. "DER RING DES NIBELUNGEN." ....- 65 -

CHAPTER V. "PARSIFAL." ....- 93 -

CHAPTER I.
THE WAGNERIAN DRAMA: ITS PROTOTYPES AND ELEMENTS.

To understand the real position which Richard Wagner occupies in the world of art, and to appreciate the significance of the achievements which have kept that world in a turmoil for two generations, it is necessary to guard against a very prevalent misconception touching him and his activities. The world knows him as an agitator and reformer, but it does not know as clearly as it ought that the object for which he labored as controversialist and composer was a reform of the opera, not a reform of music in general. Outside the theatre, it is true, he exerted a tremendous influence on the development of the musical art, but that influence he exerted only because he was a gifted musician who stood in the line of succession with the great ones who had widened the boundaries of music and struck out new paths for it—let me say Bach, Haydn, Gluck, Mozart, Beethoven, and Schumann. As a legitimate successor of these Kings by the grace of Genius, he advanced the musical art indeed, but as a reformer his activities went, not to music in its absolute forms, but to an entirely distinct and complex art-form: the modern opera. The term which Wagner invented to describe what he wished to see as the outcome of his strivings—the term which his enemies parodied so successfully that the parody has clung to the popular tongue and lingered in the popular ear, in spite of all explanation—is "The Art-work of the Future." By this "Art-work" he meant a form of theatrical entertainment in which poetry, music, pantomime, painting, and the plastic arts were to co-operate on a basis of mutual dependence—or better, perhaps, interdependence—and common aim, the inspiring purpose of all being dramatic expression. In the history of music and the drama certain strongly-marked phases are found, in which the interdependence of the elements which Wagner consorts in his Art-work can be traced; and if we look at these phases a little thoughtfully, they may help us to understand the present phase, and we may learn not only how to appreciate what Wagner has done, but also how to avoid the misconceptions which so frequently stand in the way of appreciation.

I.

Wagner, then, was a Reformer of the Opera; or, as I think it would better be put, a Regenerator of the Lyric Drama. The latter definition is to be preferred, because it presupposes the earlier existence of an art-form similar in purpose and elements (however dissimilar in scope and effectiveness it may have been) to that with which Wagner's name is identified in music's history. The spirit which created that art-form is as old as humanity; but the record of civilization shows two manifestations of it so striking that even the most cursory study ought to disclose Wagner's relationship to them. The Greek stage-plays were much more closely allied to the modern opera than to the modern drama. Music was an integral and essential element of them. So says Aristotle, adding, "and their greatest embellishment." The dramatic and lyrical elements were inseparable in Greek tragedy, which had its origin in the Dithyramb, a dance-song. The one modified the other. The cheer, the gravity, or the horror of the action were reflected at the same time in the music. While there was music also in comedy, yet, as Aristotle indicates, it was there of less importance, probably because comedy—which was really broad enough to meet the modern notions of farce—was beneath the true level of music as apprehended by the Greeks. As between the lyre and flute, the Greeks gave a vastly greater admiration to the former, as is indicated by a proverb quoted by Cicero: "As they say among the Greeks, they are flautists who cannot be citharists;" and it is significant that stringed accompaniments were given to the dithyrambic chorus when its purposes were serious, and accompaniments on the *aulos* when those purposes were of lighter character. Obviously the writers of Greek tragedy were of necessity versed in the musical art of their time. Æschylus was not merely a poet; he was also a musical composer. A fragment of a theoretical book on rhythm by Aristoxenus, a fellow-pupil with Alexander the Great of Aristotle, has been preserved to us. It is filled with lamentations over the decadence of dramatic music since the good old days of Æschylus, and accuses contemporary composers of pandering to the depraved tastes of the public, and disregarding the noble art of the Æschylean period. We know that Sophocles was a practical musician. He was taught both music and dancing by Lampros (or Lamprocles) the dithyrambist, in his time the foremost professor of these arts in Athens. It is on record that he played in two of his own dramas, taking the character of Nausikaa in the "Pluntriæ," and, in "Thamyris," that of a singer stricken blind by the Muses. In this latter role he so pleased the popular fancy that, by public vote, a portrait of him, with a cithara in his hands, was placed in the Painted Porch—a fact which finds mention in Athenæus. Another indication of his proficiency as a musician is that he wrote pæans and elegies, and a work in prose for the instruction of choral artists. It is written that Euripides, obviously less musician than poet, had to call in the aid of a composer to supply the essential music for one of his plays. Possibly this explains the fact that in his tragedies the odes are less intimately connected with the play than they are in the tragedies of Æschylus. They no longer form part of the action, and their beauty consists in their skilfulness of form rather than in the natural union of rhythm and music.

In the Greek tragedies the actors did not declaim their lines as ours do; they chanted them. The word which they used to describe what we call dramatic declamation was *emmeleia*, from *en* and *melos*, whence we get our word melody; so that they literally spoke of their plays as being spoken "in tune." Even the Attic orators, as well as the later Roman, delivered their orations musically, and, like the actors, sometimes had the help of an accompaniment on the lyre or flute to keep them in pitch. Cicero and Plutarch both relate an anecdote to the effect that Caius Gracchus once lost his pitch in the heat of an oration, and was brought back to it by a slave with an instrument, who was concealed behind him for that very purpose. In the plays the chorus sang the odes which filled the pauses between the various stages of the action; and as they sang they kept time with solemn dance-steps, moving from side to side and around an altar which stood in the centre of the space between the audience and the stage, called then, as now, the orchestra.[A] The choric odes were sung in unison, but, more richly than the declamation of the actors, they were accompanied by instruments which I believe we are justified in assuming (though it is a debated point) supplied a foundation of harmony for the vocal melody. Unfortunately, none of the music composed for these tragedies has been preserved; but we are surely justified in believing that, in spite of its simplicity (for simple it had to be to meet the demands of Greek philosophy), it was beautiful, impressive, and, in the highest degree, expressive music. No people have ever come nearer than those old Greeks to a correct estimate of the real nature of music and the role that it can and ought to be made to play in the economy of civilized life. So convinced were they of the directness and forcefulness of its appeal to the emotional part of man that they refused to divorce it from poetry, and hedged its practice about with legal restrictions, fearful that a too one-sided cultivation of it in its absolute state would tend to the development of the emotions at a cost of the rational and sterner elements on which the welfare of the individual and the community depended. Theirs was surely a lofty ideal: an art which charmed the senses while it persuaded the reason was a noble art. But it died with much else that was noble and lovely when the Romans succeeded the Greeks as arbiters of the civilized world. Under the Romans the lyric drama degenerated into mere spectacular mummery.

II.

Thus much for the first manifestation of the spirit which is exemplified in the Art-work of Richard Wagner. I have laid stress upon the Greek tragedy simply because it was the direct inspiration of the second manifestation, out of which the Art-work which Wagner reformed was evolved, through steps that are easily followed by students of modern musical history. Wherever we turn we find the genesis of the drama to be the same. I might have chosen the Hindu drama as a starting-point, and found in it the same intimate association of poetry, music, and action that characterized Greek tragedy. Or I might have pointed to the Chinese drama, and invited you to a study of that association as it has existed for thousands of years, and still exists in the theatres of the Great Pure Kingdom.

Now for the second manifestation. Towards the close of the sixteenth century dissatisfaction with the inelastic artificiality of polite music took possession of a body of scholars and musical amateurs who were in the habit of meeting for learned discussion in the house of Giovanni Bardi, Count Vernio, in Florence. Their discussions led them to formulate two aims: *First*, To give emotional expressiveness to music by putting aside polyphony, and inventing what is called the monodic style. They wrote solos for the voice with harmonic support for the instruments in the shape of chords. *Second*, They tried to revive the Greek tragedies, or, rather, to imitate them in new compositions, to which they applied their monodic music. They conceived the purpose of music to be to heighten the expressiveness of poetry, and held the play to be "the thing." To "Euridice," the first drama of the new style which was published, the composer of the music, Jacopo Peri, wrote a preface, in which he said that he had been convinced by a study of the ancients that though their dramatic declamation may not have risen to song, it was yet musically colored. This exaltation of speech he evidently thought had its basis in those variations of pitch, dynamic intensity, and vocal quality which Herbert Spencer, in his essay on the "Origin and Function of Music," shows to be the physiological results of variations of feeling, all feelings being muscular stimuli. Peri made careful observations of the inflections which mark ordinary speech, and attempted to reproduce his discoveries as faithfully as possible in the musical investiture which he gave to the poet's lines. "Soft and gentle speech he interpreted by half-spoken, half-sung tones, on a sustained instrumental bass; feelings of a deeper, emotional kind by a melody with greater intervals and a lively *tempo*, the accompanying instrumental harmonies changing more frequently."[B] He bestowed the greatest care on the rhythm of the music, making it flow along with the rhythm of the words.

These men were as revolutionary in their day as Wagner in ours, many times as intolerant, and, some will say, perhaps equally visionary. They revamped the Hellenic myths concerning the power of music, not as containing a germ of verity wrapped in an ample cloak of poetical symbolism, but as very truth. What the ancient art had been they did not know, but they did not hesitate to say that compared with it the music of their own time (the time of Palestrina and the Netherland School) was a barbarism, the creation of a people whose natural rudeness was evidenced even in their uncouth names—Okeghem, Hobrecht, etc. They could not reconcile counterpoint with the theories touching the province of music laid down by Plato; and that fact sufficed to condemn it. Count Vernio himself published a tract stating the purposes of the reformers. The first step in the process of curing the evil which had come over music, he said, should be to protect the poetical text from the musicians who, to exploit their inventions, tore the poetry to tatters, giving different voices different words to sing simultaneously. The philosophers of old—Plato in particular—had said that the melody should follow the verses of the poet and sweeten them. "When you compose, therefore," said the noble amateur, "have a care that the text remain uninjured, the words be kept intelligible, and do not permit yourselves to be carried off your feet by counterpoint, that wicked swimmer, who is swept along unresistingly by the stream, and arrives at an entirely different landing-place than he intended to make. For, as much as the soul is nobler than the body, so much nobler are words than counterpoint; and as the soul must govern the body, so counterpoint must take its laws from poetry." Caccini, who was a famous singing-master, and the first professional musician to join the Florentine coterie, made many statements in the preface to his *Nuove Musiche* which Gluck and Wagner only echoed when they came to urge their reforms. Thus he recommends the choice of a pitch which will enable the singer always to use his natural voice, so that expression may be unconstrained. He advises that the singer emancipate himself from a too strict adherence to measure, fixing, instead, the relative value of notes by consideration for the words to which they are set. More striking than either of these utterances, however, is his condemnation of the *roulades* which had come into use even before the solo style had been invented. He calls these *roulades* "Long flights" (flourishes or whirlings) of the voice (*lunghi giri di voce*); and says of them, literally: "They were not invented as being necessary to good singing, but, as I believe, to provide a certain titillation of the ears for the benefit of such as have little knowledge of what expressive singing means; for if they understood this, they would unquestionably detest these passages, since nothing is so offensive as they to expressive singing. And it is for this reason that I have said the *lunghi giri di voce* are so ill applied. I introduce them in songs which are less passionate, and, indeed, on long, not on short syllables, and in closing cadences." Caccini further advises the avoidance of artificial tones, and the use of the natural voice in order that the feelings may have expression. Wagner urges his singers to leave off the affected pathos which they are so prone to assume with the song-voice, and to enunciate, breathe, and phrase as naturally and unconstrainedly as they would if they were speaking the dialogue instead of singing it. Caccini wished the singer to emancipate himself from the fetters of musical metre, and to consult the rhythm of the words. In Wagner's vocal parts the aim is to achieve through music an increased expressiveness for the poetry, and to this end he raises it to a kind of intensified speech, which retains as much as possible of the distinctness of ordinary dialogue with its emotional capacity raised to a higher power. He desires that the melody shall spring naturally from the poetry, but also that the poetry shall "yearn" for musical expression. Caccini recognized the beauty of embellished song, but restricted the introduction of vocal flourishes to songs which were wanting in expressiveness—in other words, to songs intended merely to charm the ear. Wagner (and here I should like to correct an almost universal misconception)—Wagner never condemned beautiful singing, even in the Italian sense, except where it stands in the way of truthful, dramatic utterance. But he raises the question of nationality and tongue as one which must first of all be considered in determining how poetry is to be set to music. Deference must be paid to the genius of the language employed, and also to the vocal peculiarities of the people who are to perform and enjoy the drama. This is really Wagner's starting-point. He aims to be a national dramatist. In the Italian opera the vocal adornments, favored by the inherent softness and beauty of the Italian language, gradually usurped the first place, while dramatic motive, which had inspired the invention of the opera, dropped out of sight. For such an art there is little natural aptitude in the German, and consequently only a modicum of sympathy. Sung to florid tunes, German words become worse than unintelligible; the poetry loses its merit as speech, and the music is robbed of all its purpose and most of its charm. Believing this, and having already striven to restore naturalness of expression in the spoken drama, Wagner wrote the vocal parts of his lyric dramas so as to bring out first the force of the poetry as such.

There is one more point of resemblance between Wagner and the creators of the Italian lyric drama which I must refer to briefly. It may help us out from the sway of that prejudice which we are so prone to feel towards an innovator, to learn that in so many essentials Wagner has simply given new expression to old ideas. Already, in his "Euridice," Peri concealed his orchestra behind the scenes; but as this device was borrowed from the old Roman pantomimes, and was a general custom, I lay no stress upon it. Monteverde, who did not belong to the band of Florentine reformers, but adopted their theories and put them into practice with far greater skill than any of the originators of the new style, added to the instrumental apparatus until he had a reputation for noise with which that of Wagner, in this respect, is no circumstance. In his "Orfeo" he employed thirty-six different instruments, and it has even been suspected that he was the precursor of Wagner in the device of characterizing his personages by relegating to each a certain instrument or set of instruments. But this, I am convinced, is based on a misunderstanding. It is certain, however, that he used his instruments in such a way as to emphasize climaxes, holding some of them back until the arrival of moments in the action when their sudden entrance would have a particularly telling effect.

III.

Where does Wagner touch hands with the first creators of the art-form of which I have called him the regenerator? What are the fundamental features of his system? What were the impulses which led him out of the beaten path of opera composers? I will try to answer these questions on broad lines, keeping essential principles in view rather than trifling details.

Wagner must be associated with the Greek tragedy-writers: *First* (and foremost), because he is poet as well as musical composer. He unites in himself the same qualifications (but with the tremendous difference in degree brought about by the changed conditions) as did Æschylus.

Second. Wagner sees in the drama the highest form of art—one that unites in itself the expressive potentiality of each of the elements employed in it, raised to a still higher potency through the merit of their co-operation.

Third. Wagner believes, like the Greek tragedians, that the fittest subjects for dramatic treatment are to be found in legends and mythologies.

Fourth. Wagner believes that the elements of the lyric drama ought to be adapted to the peculiarities, and to encourage the national feeling of the people for whom it is created.

This last point is of such vast significance to the question of the degree of appreciation which Wagner's art ought to receive, and also to an understanding of his attitude towards Italian music, that I wish to emphasize it before proceeding further. Wagner is as distinctively a German dramatist as Æschylus was a Greek or Shakespeare an English. In his poetry, in his music, in the moral and physical character of his dramatic personages—in brief, in the matter and the essence of his dramas—the world must recognize the Teuton. As their spirit roots in the German heart, so their form roots in the German language. One of Wagner's most persistent aims was to reanimate a national art-spirit in Germany. The rest of the world he omitted from his consideration. Those of his dramas in which he carried out his principles in their fulness are scarcely conceivable in any other language than the German, and complete or ideal appreciation of them is possible only to persons who sympathize deeply with German feelings. His whole system, of dramatic declamation rests on the genius of the German tongue. He protests against the attempt to use the *bel canto* of the Italians in German opera, because the German language is too harsh for florid music, and German throats are not flexible enough to execute agile and mellifluous melodies. In the structure of his system there is everywhere discernible a recognition of the characteristics, physiological as well as psychological, which have always marked Teutonic races. Look at Wagner in the conduct of his polemical battle; in the vehemence of his sincerity, and the rude, sledge-hammer vigor of his manner, he is as distinctively a national type as Luther. Aside from all other considerations, such a man cannot conceive music to be mere "lascivious pleasings." To the Northern mind there has always seemed to be something vicious in the influence of Southern art and manners. It seems to feel instinctively that its vigor is preserved by periodical rebellion against Roman things, and it points as a reason and a warning example to the physical and moral degeneracy of those Goths and Franks who lost their rugged virtues by too long dalliance with the Roman colonists. "Strength before Beauty," "Truth before Convention"—these are German ideals in art as well as in morals.[C]

It is only to recognize a truth, which Wagner himself freely confessed, to say that arts and manners based on such ideals do not always appear pleasing—that, in fact, they sometimes, at first blush, at least, appear uncouth and unamiable. But that fact need not long give us pause. We have simply to recognize that beauty, like everything else so far as we are concerned, is subject to change, and that a new order of beauty, which may be called characteristic beauty, has come to the fore with a claim for recognition as a fit element in dramatic representation. Are we bound to accept as infallible the popular maxim that no matter what the state of affairs on the stage, the accompanying music must delight the ear? Suppose that a composer, utilizing the ear simply as one of the gate-ways to the higher faculties, and aiming to quicken the imagination and stir the emotions, should find a means for doing this without pleasing the ear—would his art be bad for that reason? Was the agony on the faces of the Laocoön put there by the sculptor for the purpose of pleasing the eye? Does it please the eye, or does it fascinate with a horrible fascination, and achieve the artist's real purpose by appealing through the eye to the imagination and emotions?

These questions are in the nature of argument and foreign to my immediate purpose; in the way of contrast, however, the thoughts to which they give rise will help us to appreciate one phase of the Teutonism which Wagner has impressed upon his dramas which is altogether lovely. We will look at it in both of its expositions, musical and literary, for thus we shall learn something of his constructive methods as well as his poetical impulses. I refer to the ethical idea pervading those of his dramas which, like the Greek tragedies, are based on legendary or mythical tales. The idea is that *salvation comes to humanity through the self-sacrificing love of woman.* This idea is at the bottom of the great poems and dramas of Germany; it is the main-spring of "The Flying Dutchman," "Tannhäuser," and "The Niblung's Ring;" the *chorus mysticus* which ends Goethe's "Faust" proclaims it oracularly:

"All things transitory

But as symbols are sent.

Earth's insufficiency

Here grows to event.

The Indescribable,

Here it is done.

The Woman-Soul leadeth us

Upward and on!"

In the creations of Wagner, by a singular coincidence, this beautiful idea is born simultaneously with the fundamental principle of his constructive scheme—the use of melodic phrases as symbols of the persons, passions, and principles concerned in the play. His first drama based on a legendary story is "The Flying Dutchman." The infinite longing for rest of the Wandering Jew of the sea, and the infinite pity and wondrous love of the woman who, through sacrifice of her own life, achieved for the wanderer surcease of suffering—these are the two fundamental passions of the play. The legend of the Dutchman and his doom is told in a ballad which the heroine sings in the second act of the opera; and this ballad, Wagner tells us himself, he set to music first, even before he had completed the book. It is an epitome of the drama, ethically and musically, having two significant musical themes corresponding to the longing of the Dutchman and the redeeming love of Senta. The first of these musical themes is this:

[PNG] [Listen]

The second is this:

[PNG] [Listen]

Having invented these two phrases for use simply in the ballad, Wagner tells us how he proceeded with his work:

"I had merely to develop according to their respective tendencies the various thematic germs comprised in the ballad to have, as a matter of course, the principal mental moods in definite thematic shapes before me. When a mental mood returned, its thematic expression also, as a matter of course, was repeated, since it would have been arbitrary and capricious to have sought another *motivo* so long as the object was an intelligible representation of the subject, and not a conglomeration of operatic pieces." This is Wagner's account of the genesis of the "leading motives," or, as I think they would better be called, "typical phrases," and it directs attention to a misconception of their nature and purpose which is pretty general even among the admirers of his works. They were not invented to announce the entrance of persons of the play on their stage; their duties are not those of footmen or ushers. Nor are they labels. Neither can they rightly be likened, as a German critic has declared, to the lettered ribbons issuing from the mouths of figures in mediæval pictures. They stand for deeper things—for the attributes of the play's personages; for the instruments, spiritual as well as material, used in developing the plot; for the fundamental passions of the story. If they were labels, they could only accompany the characters with which they had been associated at the outset, and this we know is not the case; in fact, in some very significant instances, they enter the score long before the characters with whom they are associated have been heard of or their existence is surmised. They are symbols, and hence arbitrary signs, but not more arbitrary than words. All language is arbitrary convention. Only the emotional elements at the bottom of it are real, absolute, universal. It would be just as easy to build up a language of musical tones capable of expressing ideas as it was to build up a language of words. In fact, though we seldom think of it, the rudiments of such a language exist. We are all familiar with some of them, or we should not involuntarily associate certain rhythms with the dance, and others with the march. A drone-bass under an oboe melody in 6-8 time would not suggest a pastoral; trumpets and drums, war; French-horn harmonies, a hunting scene; and so on. More than this, the Chinese have retained in their language a relic of the time when music was an integral element of all speech, not only of solemn and artistic speech, as we see it in the beginnings of the drama in India, Greece, and China. The meaning of many words in the monosyllabic Chinese language depends upon the musical inflection given to them in utterance. In a sense, a phrase of melody, or a chord, or a succession of chords, of harmony, is a "bow-wow word," the only kind of word universally intelligible. A great deal of music is direct in its influence upon the emotions, but it is chiefly by association of ideas that we recognize its expressiveness or significance. Sometimes hearing a melody or harmony arouses an emotion like that aroused by the contemplation of a thing. Minor harmonies, slow movements, dark tonal colorings, combine directly to put a musically susceptible person in a mood congenial to thoughts of sorrow and death; and, inversely, the experience of sorrow, or the contemplation of death, creates affinity for minor harmonies, slow movements, and dark tonal colorings. Or we recognize attributes in music possessed also by things, and we consort the music and the things, external attributes bringing descriptive music into play which excites the fancy, internal attributes calling for an exercise of the loftier faculty, imagination, to discern their meaning. A few examples in both classes will help to make my meaning plain, and I begin with the second class as the nobler of the two.

In Wagner's Niblung tragedy two of the musical phrases associated with Wotan may be taken as symbols of contrasted attributes of the god. Throughout the tragedy of which he is the hero, Wotan figures, by virtue of his supremacy among the gods, as Lord of Valhalla, and consequently as the manifest embodiment of law.

In music the first manifestation of law is in form.

It is impossible to conceive of a combination of the integral elements of music—rhythm, melody, and harmony—in a beautiful manner without some kind of form. Form means measure, order, symmetry. In music more than in any art it is essential to the existence of the loftiest attribute of beauty, which is repose—an attribute whose divine character Ruskin proclaimed when he defined it as "the 'I am' contradistinguished from the 'I become;' the sign alike of the supreme knowledge which is incapable of surprise, the supreme power which is incapable of labor, the supreme volition which is incapable of change." Now what are the musical qualities of which Wagner makes use in order to symbolize the wielder of supreme power? Here is the phrase whose innate nobility and beauty appear to best advantage at the opening of the second scene in "Das Rheingold:"

[PNG] [Listen]

The melody is built out of the intervals of the common chord—the triad—the starting-point of harmony, its first and most pervasive law. This chord, too, supplies the harmonic structure. Its instrumentation (for four tubas with peculiarly orotund voices, specially constructed for Wagner) is unvarying, calm, stately, majestic, dignified, reposeful. Thus does Wagner symbolize musically the chief deity and chief personage of his tragedy in his character as Lord of Valhalla. But through the operation of the curse to which he became subject when he took the baneful ring, another character than that of a supreme god is forced upon Wotan. He has plotted to regain the ring, and restore it to the original owners of the magic gold. He has begotten a new race, the Volsungs, to execute a purpose which, as the representative of law, he is restrained himself from executing. He becomes a wanderer over the face of the earth, a mere spectator of the development of his foolish plot. How is this new character symbolized? Note the music which accompanies Wotan when, disguised as the Wanderer, he enters Mime's cavern smithy in the second scene of "Siegfried:"

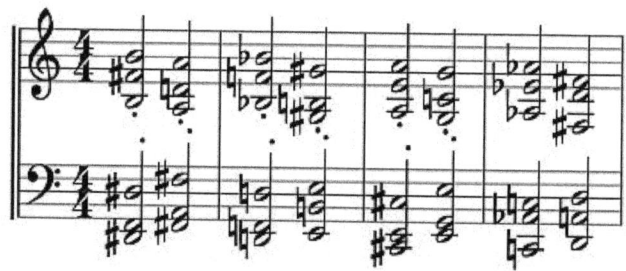

[PNG] [Listen]

The fundamental harmonies are retained. The solemn instrumental color is held fast. The dignity of the chord progressions is still there. What, then, is gone? *The element of repose.* The harmonies are still triads, but tonality, with its benison of restfulness, has been sacrificed. The phrase is in no key, or rather it is in as many keys as there are chords. There is another beautiful instance in which, by the same means, a deprivation which one of the personages of the play undergoes is made plain to the listener. Note the descending series of chords which follows Wotan's kiss depriving Brünnhilde of her divinity, just after he has spoken his pathetic farewell, and just before the orchestra begins its lullaby, in the final scene of "Die Walküre." Here the loss of divine attributes in the disobedient goddess is published by absence of fixed tonality in the chords which accompany the visible signs of her punishment.

In the last two examples we have been called on to observe how changes in character and loss of attributes are delineated by departure of tonality. I will now cite a case in which not the attributes of a personage, but the property of a thing, is the composer's objective point. The case is a striking one, for it is a supernatural property which is to be brought to the notice of the listener, the power of the *Tarnhelm* (the familiar cap of darkness of folk-lore) to render its wearer invisible. The musical symbol of this magical apparatus in the Niblung tragedy is this:

[PNG] [Listen]

This phrase is not often used, but whenever it occurs in the music its mysteriousness arrests attention. What is the source of that mysteriousness? Nothing else than indefiniteness, vagueness of mode. The closing harmony is an empty fifth; we do not know whether it is major or minor, because the determining interval is lacking. Supply a major third and it is major, a minor third and it is minor; in either case, however, the mystical property of the phrase, the element which establishes its propriety, vanishes.

There are many of these typical phrases primarily associated with personages, whose delineation goes to moods and moral traits. There are others that are frankly delineative of externals. The giants in "Das Rheingold" are the representatives of brute force. They are heavy-witted as well as heavy-footed, and their stupidity and clumsiness are aptly characterized in their melody:

(*Fasolt and Fafner, of gigantic stature, armed with strong staves, enter.*)

[PNG] [Listen]

The Niblungs are the antipodes in character of the giants—cunning, resourceful, industrious. Intellectually they are schemers and tricksters; by occupation they are smiths. Wagner delineates these activities, the mental as well as the manual, in the orchestral introduction to "Siegfried." A descending figure (*a*), (two thirds at the interval of a seventh) characterizes the brooding thoughtfulness, the cogitation of Mime; the fact that the dwarf is a Niblung Wagner publishes by means of a rhythmical phrase like the pounding of hammers (*b*):

[PNG] [Listen]

Sometimes Wagner becomes frankly delineative or descriptive, utilizing imitation of nature where it will be effective, as in the phrases associated with the Rhine and its denizens—the nixies whom he calls Daughters of the Rhine. The slow undulation of water in its depths, the flux and reflux of the element, the ripples on its surface, the motions of the swimmers, are all pictured to the ear (if I may be permitted to say so) in the melodies of the Rhine and the nixies whose home the river is, and the changes of time and treatment to which those melodies are subjected. The fitful, flickering, crackling crepitation of fire furnishes a suggestion for the phrase which is typical of Loge, the fire-god, whether he appears in his elemental form, as in the finale of "Die Walküre," or bodily as the incarnation of the spirit of mischief in "Das Rheingold:"

[PNG] [Listen]

In describing how he proceeded in the composition of "The Flying Dutchman," Wagner says that when a mental mood recurred for which he had once found thematic expression, that expression was repeated. He speaks here only of moods, but he extended the principle involved to the whole apparatus of the drama—its secret impulses as well as its external agencies. These agencies, in their physical manifestation, moreover, are sometimes anticipated by the appearance in the music of the melodic phrases which typify them; but this never happens unless they are spiritually present in the drama. This is what I have called the use of the themes for prophecy, and to me it seems one of the most beautiful features of Wagner's constructive scheme. Let me illustrate: the sword, which is the instrument designed by Wotan for the working-out of his plot for the return of the baneful ring to its original owners, for itself and as a symbol of the race of demi-gods who were to be endowed with it; Siegfried, the hero who is to be the vessel chosen, not by Wotan but by fate in the prevision of Brünnhilde, to execute the purposes of the god; Brünnhilde herself, not as a goddess but in the character of loving woman willing and able to make the redeeming sacrifice; all these are prefigured in the drama by the entrance of their typical phrases long before the action permits their physical appearance. They are seen by the prophetic vision of certain personages of the play and manifested to us through the music. Thus: the sword phrase appears in the orchestral postlude of "Das Rheingold" at the moment when Wotan, crossing the Rainbow-bridge with the members of his divine household, stops in thought and conceives the plot which is worked out in the tragedy proper; the phrase typical of the heroic character of Siegfried accompanies Brünnhilde's prediction to Sieglinde that she shall give birth to "the loftiest hero in the world," in the drama "Die Walküre;" in giving voice to her gratitude, Sieglinde, in turn, hails Brünnhilde as the representative of the redeeming principle of the tragedy, Goethe's "Ewig-Weibliche," by using a melody which examination shows to be an augmentation of the melodic symbol of Brünnhilde when she appears as mere woman in the last drama of the trilogy.

Let this suffice as an exhibition of Wagner's method of inventing and introducing the melodic material out of which he weaves his fabric, while we look at some of the principles applied in its use. His system rests upon the development of these themes, not according to the laws of the symphony, but in harmony with the dramatic spirit of the text. The orchestra is the vehicle of this development. It is pre-eminently the expositor of the drama. It has acquired some of the functions of the Greek chorus, in that it takes part in the action to publish that which is beyond the capacity of the personages alone to utter. The music of the instruments is the voice of the fate, the conscience, and the will concerned in the drama. To those who wish to listen, it unfolds, unerringly, the thoughts, motives, and purpose of the personages, and lays bare the mysteries of the plot and counter-plot. As the passions and purposes of the drama grow complex, the musical texture, into which the themes which typify those passions and purposes enter, grows complex and heterogeneous. The most obvious factors in this development are changes of mode, harmony, rhythm, time, and orchestration. A single illustration must here suffice. By applying the principle of augmentation to a phrase, in the three phases of melodic, harmonic, and instrumental structure, Wagner illustrates the tragic growth of Siegfried in the Niblung tragedy. When the hero is merely a high-spirited lad, roaming through the forest and associating with its denizens, the phrase appears as the call which he blows upon his hunting-horn:

[PNG] [Listen]

When he has entered upon man's estate, has awakened Brünnhilde from her long sleep, learned wisdom from her teaching, donned her armor, and is about to set out in quest of adventure, the typical phrase which greets him has taken on this form:

[PNG] [Listen]

Finally, the phrase is metamorphosed into that thrilling pæan at the climax of the Death March, to indicate which is impossible by means of pianoforte transcription:

[PNG] [Listen]

IV.

From the beginning of his career Wagner wrote his own librettos; but it is only in "Tristan und Isolde," "Die Meistersinger," "Der Ring des Nibelungen," and "Parsifal" that he realized his conception of what the poet-composer should be. The starting-point of his reformatory ideas was that music had usurped a place which does not belong to it in the lyric drama. It should be a means, and had become the aim. As an æsthetic principle, he contended that it lies in the nature of music to be not the end, but a medium, of dramatic expression. He therefore reversed the old relations of librettist and composer, and made music, which can only address itself to the emotions and imagination, dependent for form, spirit, and character on the poetry, which appeals to reason. Each art when isolated has a restricted range of expression; but in the Wagnerian drama each contributes a complement and helps it to convey all its meanings and intentions without the help of a frequently untrustworthy imagination. In elaborating his theory, Wagner held that as a poetical form of expression rhyme is useless in music, because it not only implies identity of vowel-sounds, but also of the succeeding consonants, which are lost by the singer's need of dwelling on the vowels. The initial consonant, however, cannot be lost in song, because it is that which stamps its physiognomy on the word, and repetition creating a sort of musical cadence which is agreeable to the ear, Wagner desired alliteration to be substituted for rhyme in the chief parts of his verse. From the verse-melody thus obtained he wished the musical melody to spring, words and music becoming lovingly merged in each other, each sacrificing enough of selfishness to make the union possible. To what I have already said about the nature of the typical phrases I wish to add this as a résumé of their purpose: In every drama there are employed certain dramatic and ethical principles as well as agencies. The development of these principles in the conduct and words of the personages, the employment of the agencies, give us the action and significance of the play. For these principles and agents Wagner provides musical symbols. The nature of the principles, the character of the agents, explain the form and spirit of the symbols; the symbols, in turn, sometimes help us to understand the real nature of the things symbolized. If we have grasped the fundamental ideas of a drama, therefore, and appreciated the fitness of their symbols, we shall have penetrated near to the heart of the Art-work. But it cannot be too forcibly urged that if we confine our study of Wagner to the forms and names of the phrases out of which he constructs his musical fabric, we shall at the last have enriched our minds with a thematic catalogue and—nothing else. We shall remain guiltless of knowledge unless we learn something of the nature of those phrases by noting the attributes which lend them propriety and fitness, and can recognize, measurably at least, the reasons for their introduction and development. Those attributes give character and mood to the music constructed out of the phrases. If we are able to feel the mood we need not care how the phrases which produce it have been labelled. If we do not feel the mood we may memorize the whole thematic catalogue of Wolzogen and have our labor for our pains. It would be better to know nothing about the phrases and content one's self with simple sensuous enjoyment than to spend one's time answering the baldest of all the riddles of Wagner's orchestra: "What am I playing now?"

The ultimate question concerning the correctness or effectiveness of Wagner's system of composition must, of course, be answered along with the question, "Does the composition, as a whole, touch the emotions, quicken the fancy, fire the imagination?" If it does these things, we may, to a great extent, if we wish, get along without the intellectual processes of reflection and comparison, which are conditioned upon a recognition of the themes and their uses. But if we put aside this intellectual activity, we shall deprive ourselves, among other things, of the pleasure which it is the province of memory to give; and the exercise of memory is called for by music much more urgently than by any other art, because of its volatile nature and the role which repetition plays in it.

Nothing could have demonstrated more perfectly the righteousness of Wagner's claim to the title of poet than his acceptance of the Greek theory that the legends and myths of a people are the fittest subjects for dramatic treatment, unless it be the manner in which he has reshaped his material in order to infuse it with that deep ethical principle to which reference has several times been made. In "The Flying Dutchman," "The Niblung's Ring," and "Tannhäuser," the idea is practically his creation. In the last of these three dramas it is evolved out of the simple episode in the parent-legend of the death of Lisaura, whose heart broke when her knight went to kiss the Queen of Love and Beauty. The dissolute knight of the old story Wagner in turn metamorphoses into a type of manhood "in its passionate desires and ideal aspirations"—like the Faust of Goethe. All the magnificent energy of an ideal man is brought forward in the poet's conception, but it is an energy which is shattered in its fluctuation between sensual delights and ideal aspirations, respectively typified in the Venus and the Elizabeth of the play. Here is the contradiction against which he was shattered as the heroes of Greek tragedy were shattered on the rock of implacable Fate. But the transcendent beauty of the modern drama is lent by the ethical idea of salvation through the love of pure woman—a salvation touching which no one can be in doubt when Tannhäuser sinks lifeless beside the bier of the atoning saint, and Venus's cries of woe are swallowed up by the pious canticle of the returning pilgrims.

FOOTNOTES:

[A] For popular purposes there is no harm in letting this statement stand as made. Of course the reference goes only to the Greek theatre in its latest form, the evolution of which is indicated, perhaps, in the comparative weakness of the bond which unites the chorus to the action in Euripides. The orchestra was, in fact, the centre around which all the rest, the *theatron* and the *skēnē*, were gradually grouped. In the antique festal plays the principal feature was the dance in a circle around the *thymele*, or altar of Dionysus. It was only by a slow process that the actor came to be thought of as anywise distinguished from his companions. As generally in ancient art priority was indicated by height, there is here a reason for the tragic *cothurnus*, which might be said to be an inexplicable deformity on any other theory; for it was only by putting them on stilts, so to speak, that it was possible to indicate the participants in the dialogue as apart from the general rout of dancing worshippers. Even in the time of the three great dramatic writers, it seems probable, disturbing as such an idea may be to popular impressions, that some, if not all, plays were performed without any stage. The word *skēnē* (tent) points to a temporary structure, used in the first place, perhaps, as a shrine for the symbols and properties of the god (like the Tabernacle of the Israelites), then as the dressing-room of the actors; it was succeeded by the temple when the place had become consecrated to the worship of Dionysus, then by the structures suited to a given play, and finally by a permanent stage, which gradually encroached on the space that had once belonged to the orchestra. These conclusions, at least, seem to be borne out by the discoveries and arguments of Dörpfeld.

[B] Naumann's *History of Music*, vol. i., p. 524.

[C] *Mephist.* Du weisst wohl nicht, mein Freund, wie grob du bist?
Bac. Im Deutschen lügt man wenn man höflich ist.

GOETHE. "Faust," Part II., Act 2, Sc. 1.

CHAPTER II.
"TRISTAN UND ISOLDE."

A vassal is sent to woo a beauteous princess for his lord. While he is bringing her home the two, by accident, drink a love-potion, and ever thereafter their hearts are fettered together. In the mid-day of delirious joy, in the midnight of deepest woe, and through all the emotional hours between, their thoughts are only of each other, for each other. Meanwhile the princess has become the vassal's queen. Then the wicked love of the pair is discovered, and the knight is obliged to seek safety in a foreign land. There (strange note this to our ears) he marries another princess whose name is like that of his love, save for the addition "With the White Hand;" but when wounded unto death he sends across the water for her who is still his true love, that she come and be his healer. The ship which is sent to bring her is to bear white sails on its return if successful in the mission; black, if not. Day after day the knight waits for the coming of his love—while the lamp of his life burns lower and lower. At length the sails of the ship appear on the distant horizon. The knight is now too weak himself to look. "White or black?" he asks of his wife. "Black," replies she, jealousy prompting the falsehood; and the knight's heart-strings snap in twain just as his love steps over the threshold of his chamber. Oh, the pity of it! for with the lady is her lord, who, having learned the story of the fateful potion, has come to unite the lovers. Then the queen, too, dies, and the remorseful king buries the lovers in a common grave, from whose caressing sod spring a rose-bush and a vine, and intertwine so curiously that none may separate them.

Here, in its simple forms, is the tale which half a millennium of poets have celebrated as the High Song of Love, the canticle of all canticles which hymn the universal passion. British bards, French *trouvères*, and German *Minnesinger*, while they sang of the joys and sorrows of humanity, united in holding up Sir Tristram and La beale Isoud as the supreme type of lovers. To-day our poets, writing under the influence of social and moral systems, radically different from those which surrounded the original singers, send back the perennial note with fervor. But the moralist shakes his head, sinks into perplexed brooding, or launches the thunders of his righteous wrath against the storied lovers and their sin. We wish to study the manner in which a great dramatic poet of our day has presented this profoundly tragical yet universally fascinating tale. Must we confront the problem and seek to reconcile the paradox created by the attitudes of poet and moralist? Or may we put aside the phenomenon as one whose interpretation is to be left to each individual's notions of the True, the Beautiful, and the Good, and address ourselves directly to a study of the drama as a work of art regardless of its ethical phases? Eventually, I am inclined to believe, we shall be obliged to do the latter; but as appreciation of what the poet-composer has done depends upon an understanding of his purposes, and this again upon a discovery of the elements of the legend which seemed to him potential, we are compelled to make at least a cursory survey of some of the phases through which the story has gone in the progress of time; for each poet, passing the original metal through the fires of his imagination, brought it forth changed in color and enriched with new designs. In the new color and adornments we study something of the social institutions and moral and intellectual habits of the poet's time, these being superimposed on the original idea embodied in the fundamental story. In one of the beautiful tales of Northern mythology (a tale in which I am tempted to think a relic of the primitive Tristram myth may one day be found) we are told how Skirnir cunningly stole the reflection of Frey's sunny face from the surface of a brook, and imprisoned it in his drinking-horn that he might pour it out into Gerd's cup, and by its beauty win the heart of the giantess for the lord for whom, like Tristan, he had gone a-wooing. A legend which lives to be retold often, is like the reflection of Frey's face in this beautiful allegory; each poet who uses it spreads it upon a mirror which not only reflects the original picture, but also the environment of the relator. It will be necessary to remember this when we attempt an inquiry into the morals of Wagner's drama.

I.

To readers of English literature opportunities to acquaint themselves with the legend which is the basis of Wagner's drama have been given by Sir Thomas Malory, Matthew Arnold, Tennyson, and Swinburne, to say nothing of critics and commentators. The story is of Keltic origin, and is supposed to have got into the mouths of the German *Minnesinger* by way of France. The most admirable as well as complete version extant is the epic poem of Gottfried von Strassburg, written in the thirteenth century. Sir Walter Scott, who was deeply interested in the literary history of the tale, in 1804 edited a metrical version of it from a manuscript said to be the production of Thomas the Rhymer, who lived about a century after Gottfried, if, indeed, he lived at all. From this manuscript Scott argued in favor of a Welsh source for the romance instead of a Norman, as was then generally accepted. The author of the German epic followed a French version, as was customary with the *Minnesinger* of his period. Tennyson's share in the exposition is exceedingly scant and wholly valueless. It is found in the poem, "The Last Tournament," one of the "Idyls of the King." Arnold's is much more interesting. He treats directly of the outcome of the tragedy in his poem "Tristram and Iseult," and indirectly relates nearly all that is essential to an understanding of the story. His poem presents the death scene of Tristram in Brittany, with the fanciful imaginings of the dying man while waiting for the coming of Iseult, who has been summoned from Tintagel. The whole tale is related by Swinburne in his "Tristram of Lyonesse."

The names of the chief personages in the romance vary slightly in the different German and English versions, but the variations need lead no one astray. Wagner's Tristan is otherwise known as Sir Tristrem and Tristram. All derive the name from the French word *triste*, and find in it a premonition of his fate. Thus Arnold:

"Son," she said, "thy name shall be of sorrow;
Tristram art thou called for my death's sake."

The poet speaks of the hero's dying mother. So also Swinburne:

"The name his mother, dying as he was born,
Made out of sorrow in very sorrow's scorn,
And set it on him smiling in her sight,
Tristram."

Isolde is variously Iseult, Ysolt, Isoud, and Ysonde; Brangäne is Brangwain and Brenqwain; Kurwenal, Gouvernayle. The changes in orthographical physiognomy are trifling and easily recognized.

It cannot be amiss to call attention to several deviations in Wagner's drama from the legend as it has been handed down by the poets. The majority of these deviations will be found to be full of significance. At the outset we are confronted with the chief of these. In all the other versions the love-potion is drunk by Tristan and Isolde by mistake. In Mr. Swinburne's poem Tristram toils at the oars,

"More mightily than any wearier three,"

and when he rests, calls for a drink,

"Saying: 'Iseult, for all dear love's labor's sake,
Give me to drink, and give me for a pledge
The touch of four lips on the beaker's edge'."

Iseult's maid, Brangwain, is asleep, and the Princess, not wishing to awake her, herself looks for wine and finds a curious cup hid in the maid's bosom. She thinks its contents wine and drinks, and hands it to Tristram to drink.

It is the love-draught prepared by Queen Iseult and intrusted to Brangwain, to be by her sacredly guarded and given to Mark and Iseult on their wedding night. Mr. Arnold also has these lovers drink unwittingly

"——that spiced magic draught

Which since then forever rolls

Through their blood and binds their souls,

Working love, but working teen."

In this respect both English poets follow the German epic of Gottfried von Strassburg. The dramatic significance of Wagner's variation can be reserved for discussion hereafter. Its value as intensifying the character of Isolde is obvious at a glance.

Tennyson omits all mention of the love-potion, and permits us to imagine Tristram and Iseult as a couple of ordinary sinners, the former's doctrines on the subject being published in lines like these:

"Free love—free field—we love but while we may;

The woods are hush'd, their music is no more:

The leaf is dead, the yearning passed away:

New leaf, new life—the days of frost are o'er:

New life, new love to suit the newer day:

New loves are sweet as those that went before;

Free love—free field—we love but while we may."

The next important variation (I do not speak of omissions which are inevitable in throwing an epic into dramatic form) is in the scene which follows the discovery of the lovers by King Marke. To discuss this in all its bearings would require more space than I shall care to employ for the purpose, but it is well to know it. The wronged Marke of Wagner, some will say as many have said, is not wronged at all since he chooses to remain inactive, whereas the popular impulse is illustrated in Tennyson's version, where Mark cleaves Tristram to the brain on discovering his treachery. But the Marke of Gottfried and the Mark of Swinburne are scarcely more comprehensible in their conduct than Wagner's Marke. In Gottfried's epic, after the king has repeatedly sent the lovers away and taken them back again, he is finally convinced of their guilt. But before he takes action against Tristan, the latter escapes. In Swinburne, Tristram is taken and led towards the chapel for trial. On the road he wrenches a sword from Moraunt's hands, kills him and ten knights more, leaps into the sea from a cliff, and escapes, aided by Gouvernayle.

In his last act, Wagner has proceeded with the utmost freedom, as in all respects he had a right to do, since no authentic version of the close of the legend has been preserved. Karl Simrock, following the old English "Sir Tristrem," appended to his translation into modern German of Gottfried's epic the episode of Tristan's life in Brittany with a second Isolt, called Isolt of the White Hand. Being low with a wound received in combat, Tristan sends for the first Isolt, cautioning his brother-in-law (as Ægeus cautioned Theseus in Greek story), who goes on the mission, to hoist white sails on returning if successful, black if not. Isolt of the White Hand, who is watching for the return of the ship, moved by jealousy, announces that the sails are black, and Tristan dies just as Isolt enters the chamber. This version Swinburne follows, but Arnold adds a beautiful touch to the old legend by making the second Iseult tend her husband with unflinching love and unfailing fidelity, even while she awaits the coming of her rival. Arnold gives Tristram and the second Iseult a family of children; Swinburne keeps the latter a "maiden wife." Bayard Taylor, in writing about Gottfried's epic, almost angrily refuses to believe that Iseult of the White Hand killed her knight by the falsehood about the sails. Wagner saves himself this embarrassment, and ennobles his hero by omitting the second Isolde from the play altogether, a proceeding which not only brings the tale into greater sympathy with modern ideas of love, but also serves marvellously to exalt the passion of the lovers.

II.

Wagner tells the story of the tragedy in three acts. Few dramas have so little to offer in the way of action, if by action we are to understand incident and diversity of situation. At Bayreuth, in the summer of 1886, Mr. Seidl characterized it very aptly as consisting in each of its three acts as merely preparation, expectation and meeting of the ill-starred lovers. Yet I doubt not that many will agree with me, that the effect of the tragedy upon a listener is that of a play surcharged with significant occurrence. The explanation of this is to be found in the fact that music which has a high degree of emotional expressiveness makes us forget the paucity of external incident, by diverting interest from externals to the play of passion going on in the hearts of the personages. This play is presented to us freed from every vestige of spectacular integument in the instrumental prelude to the drama. I want to lay stress on this statement. It is the passion of the lovers to which the composer wishes to direct our attention at the outset, and to do this most effectively he constructs his musical "argument of the play" out of melodic phrases which have purely a psychological significance. There is considerable music of the kind that I will call scenic in the score of "Tristan und Isolde," but none of it is introduced in the prelude, which for that reason appeals much more directly to the emotions and the lofty faculty of imagination than it does to the fancy. It is true that this makes the task of analytical study more difficult, but for this there is compensation in the fact that enjoyment of its beauties and apprehension of its purposes do not require the intellectual activity conditioned by a following of its typical phrases through the web and woof of the composition. This is characteristic of the entire score of the drama. More than any other of the dramas of Wagner, with the possible exception of "Die Meistersinger," it shows the spontaneity in artistic creation, without which a real art-work cannot come into existence. Wagner himself expressed a preference for "Tristan" over others of his works, and based it on the solid ground that in the composition of its score he had proceeded without thought of his own theories; in other words, he worked spontaneously and not reflectively. The result is strikingly noticeable in the fact that, though there are comparatively few typical melodies in the score, one is much less inclined to dissect it for the pleasure which such a process brings than any other of his scores. The direct, sensuous, and emotional appeal is sufficient. Yet we know that it is a perfect and complete exemplification of his theories.

To come back to the prelude:

An ardent longing for the unattainable; a consuming hunger

"——which doth make

The meat it feeds on;"

a desire that cannot be quenched, yet will not despair; finally, at the lowest ebb of the sweet agony, the promise of an end of suffering, in self-forgetfulness, oblivion, annihilation of individual identity, and hence in a blending or union of identity—these, according to Wagner's exposition and the play itself, are the elements which are prefigured in the instrumental introduction. What are their musical symbols?

The fundamental theme of the drama, the kernel of its musical development, is the phrase which we hear at the beginning of the prelude:

[PNG] [Listen]

Brief as this is, it illustrates one step in the melodic development, in respect of which "Tristan und Isolde" is Wagner's most marvellous achievement. It is a unit, in so far as it stands for the passion of the pair, in both its aspects of blissful longing and infinite suffering, but it is nevertheless already complex. It is two-voiced. One voice descends chromatically, the other (beginning with the third measure) ascends by similar degrees. A figure like that used in music to indicate a *crescendo*,

presents a symbol of duality in unity for the eye like that of this phrase for the ear. How simple yet profound is the idea that all the conflicting passions of the drama are one in origin and in nature. Am I becoming fantastical in thinking that Wagner purposed that this philosophical concept should be stated in the basic material of his music? I think not; but if there is a haunting fear that way it may be dissipated by looking a little further into the prelude. After a brief development of this first musical thought by means of repetition on various degrees of the scale and changes of instrumental color, two new phrases are reached. The first:

[PNG] [Listen]

followed immediately by:

[PNG] [Listen]

Now, let us stop to note some resemblances, and from significant portions of the play derive a meaning for our symbols. In this we cannot be helped, as we sometimes are, by natural likenesses. These melodies are not imitative or delineative of external things; they are the result of efforts to give expression to soul-states. At the beginning of Scene 5, Act I., the entrance of Tristan is proclaimed in a manner that leaves no doubt as to the meaning of the first of the two phrases now under investigation. The melody there appears extended, in augmentation, as the musicians say. It stands for the hero of the tragedy. The genesis of the love of Tristan and Isolde must next be studied. That love antedated the beginning of our tragedy. Isolde relates the story of its beginning to her maid. Disguised as a harper, Tristan had come to Ireland to be healed of a wound received in battle with Isolde's betrothed, whom he had killed. Isolde nursed him, but before he was completely restored to health she discovered that the edge of his sword was broken, and that a splinter of steel taken from the head of her dead lover fitted into the nick. The slayer of her betrothed lay before her. She raised the sword to avenge his death, but as she was about to strike, Tristan turned his glance upon her. He looked not at the threatening sword, but into her eyes, and in a moment her heart was empty of anger. Hatred had given place to love. Note here that while Wagner uses that silly apparatus of mediæval romance, the philter, it is not as the creator or provoker of love; that is born without the aid of magic other than Nature's. "He looked into my eyes," says Isolde, and immediately the tender second phrase is uttered by the orchestra. It is thus that this phrase is identified with the glance which aroused Isolde's love.

The material which has now been marshalled is practically all that is contained in the prelude; but there are two modifications of the fundamental phrase which ought to be noticed. One of these, frequently treated responsively by the instruments to build up a climax,

[PNG] [Listen]

seems to depict the gradual recognition by the lovers of the state into which the potion has plunged them. The other is a harmonized inversion of the same figure,

[PNG] [Listen]

to which an added character is given by the jubilant ascent of thirty-second notes, and which, from several climactic portions of the drama, we discover to be significant of the lovers' joyful defiance of death—a sentiment which will be better understood after the philosophy of the tragedy has been studied.

Wagner has himself given us an exposition of this prelude. In one of his writings, after rehearsing the legend down to the drinking of the fateful potion, he says:

"Now there is no end to the yearning, the longing, the delight, and the misery of love. World, might, fame, splendor, honor, knighthood, truth, and friendship all vanish like a baseless dream. Only one thing survives: desire, desire unquenchable, and ever freshly manifested longing—thirst and yearning. One only redemption: death, the sinking into oblivion, the sleep from which there is no awaking!

"The musician who chose this theme for the prelude to his love-drama, as he felt that he was here in the boundless realm of the very element of music, could only have one care: how he should set bounds to his fancy; for the exhaustion of the theme was impossible. Thus he took once for all this insatiable desire; in long-drawn accents it surges up, from its first timid confession, its softest attraction, through throbbing sighs, hope and pain, laments and wishes, delight and torment, up to the mightiest onslaught, the most powerful endeavor to find the breach which shall open to the heart the path to the ocean of the endless joy of love. In vain! Its power spent, the heart sinks back to thirst with desire, with desire unfulfilled, as each fruition only brings forth seeds of fresh desire, till, at last, in the depth of its exhaustion, the starting eye sees the glimmering of the highest bliss of attainment. It is the ecstasy of dying, of the surrender of being, of the final redemption into that wondrous realm from which we wander farthest when we strive to take it by force. Shall we call this Death? Is it not rather the wonder-world of Night, out of which, so says the story, the ivy and the vine sprang forth in tight embrace o'er the tomb of Tristan and Isolde?"

III.

We are on board a mediæval ship within a few hours' voyage of Cornwall, whither Tristan, knight and vassal, is bearing Isolde as bride of King Marke. Isolde is an Irish princess, daughter of a queen of like name with herself. The first scene discloses her to be a woman of most tumultuous passion. Hearing the cheery song of a sailor, she bursts forth like a tempest and declares to her maid, Brangäne, that she will never set foot on Cornwall's shore. She deplores the degeneracy of her mother's sorcery, which can only brew balsamic potions instead of commanding the elements; and she wildly invokes wind and waves to dash the ship to pieces. Brangäne pleads to know the cause of her mistress's disquiet—what I have already related of the previous meeting between the princess and King Marke's ambassador.

After telling this tale to Brangäne, Isolde sends the maid to summon Tristan to her presence, but the knight refuses to leave the helm until he has brought the ship into harbor, and his squire, Kurwenal, incensed at the tone addressed by the princess to one who in his eyes is the greatest of heroes, as answer to the summons sings a stave of a popular ballad which recounts the killing of Morold and the liberation of Cornwall by his master. The refusal completes the desperation of Isolde. Outraged love, injured personal and national pride (for she imagines that he who had relieved Cornwall from tribute to Ireland was now gratifying his ambition by bringing her as Ireland's tribute to Cornwall), detestation of a loveless marriage to "Cornwall's weary king," a thousand fierce but indefinable emotions are seething in her heart. She resolves to die, and to drag Tristan down to death with her. Brangäne unwittingly shows the way. She tries to quiet her mistress's fears of the dangers of a loveless marriage by telling her of a magic potion brewed by the queen-mother with which she will firmly attach Marke to his bride. Thus innocently she takes the first step towards precipitating the catastrophe. Isolde demands to see the casket of magical philters, and finds that it also contains a deadly poison. Kurwenal enters to announce that the ship is in harbor, and Tristan desires her to prepare for the landing. Isolde sends back greetings and a message that before she will permit the knight to escort her before the king he must obtain from her forgiveness for unforgiven guilt. Tristan obeys this second summons, and in justification of his conduct in keeping himself aloof during the voyage he, with great dignity, pleads his duty towards good morals, custom, and his king. Isolde reminds him of the wrong done her in the slaying of her lover and her right to the vengeance which once she had renounced. Tristan yields the right, and offers her his sword and breast, but Isolde replies that she cannot appear before King Marke as the slayer of his foremost knight, and proposes that he drink a cup of reconciliation. Tristan sees one-half her purpose, and chivalrously consents to pledge her in what he knows to be poison. Isolde calls for the cup which she had commanded Brangäne to prepare, and when Tristan has drunk part of its contents she wrenches it from his hand and drains it to the bottom. Thus they meet their doom, which is not death and surcease of sorrow, but life and misery, for Brangäne had disobeyed her mistress out of her love and mixed a love-potion instead of a death draught. A moment of bewilderment, and the two fated ones are in each other's arms, pouring out an ecstasy of passion; then the maids of honor robe Isolde to receive King Marke, who is coming on board to greet his bride.

These are the dramatic contents of the first act, whose musical investiture is now to be looked at a little analytically. At the outset there is an example of the skill with which Wagner employs the charm of contrast. I have said that the music of the prelude is not scenic—it aims at moods and passions, not at pictures. The drama opens with music of the other kind. As the curtain is withdrawn we see within the tent erected for Isolde on the deck of the ship. Hangings conceal all else from view; but the first music which we hear is the voice of an unseen sailor at the mast-head, who sings to the winds that are blowing him away from his wild Irish sweetheart. The melody has a most insinuating charm, especially its principal phrase:

[PNG] [Listen]

There is something of the buoyant roll of the ship and the freshness of sea-breezes about it. It plunges us at once into the scenic situation, puts us on shipboard, and helps us to share in the pleasurable sensations of the voyage to Cornwall, especially when, a moment later, it accompanies and amplifies Brangäne's account of the happy progress of the voyage. Scarcely have we surrendered ourselves to this pleasure, however, before Isolde's outburst of rage turns our attention from the scenes to the personages of the play. What was innocent delight to the singer and to us (who are now playing sympathetically along in the drama) has somehow loosened an emotional tempest in the heart of the passenger most concerned in that voyage. Suddenly, as we listen to her imprecations, the whole past of the heroine is revealed—she stands before us, not the inexperienced, unconcerned princess of the other poems, but a fully developed woman, a furious woman, a tragic heroine ripe for destruction. It is a favorite device of poets and musicians—of all creative artists, indeed—to invite Nature to take part in the play of their creations. We think a thunder-storm the proper accompaniment of a murder, and balmy sunshine of a wedding. Here the breezy sea-music has provoked a storm of passion, and the composer permits the enraged princess to lash it into a fury. To suit her mood he invokes dark clouds to obscure the sunshine of its tonality, sends harsh harmonies hurtling among the simple chords that sounded its original innocency, and stirs up a whirlwind out of its first quiet movement. But when, a few moments later, Isolde has checked her wild passion, the music settles back into its original quietude, and in time with its measured pulsations we see the sailors pulling upon the ship's tackle. Now it sings its "Yo-heave-ho!" as decorously as any shanty-song.

I have referred to the duality in unity of the fundamental idea in the music of the drama. A study of the scene in which Isolde resolves upon the double crime of murder and suicide will disclose how relation in thought, emotion, and dramatic motive is expressed by relation in musical symbol. The symbol of longing contained in the fundamental phrase shows ascent in chromatic degrees. Observe, now, that in Act I., Scene 3, the sufferings of the wounded Tristan are depicted in a theme composed wholly of descending half-steps,

[PNG] [Listen]

and note, too, that the closing cadence of the short phrase which stands for the love-glance is a downward leap of seven degrees. In this phrase, as we first hear it, there is much tenderness and gentle happiness; but in the glance there was the phantom of that Life-in-Death who won Coleridge's Ancient Mariner from the grisly skeleton in their awful game of dice. Though we do not suspect it, at first, that downward leap of a seventh is an ominous symbol—the symbol of Fate, which might have been heard under the yearning voices of the prelude, and is now proclaimed by the gloomy basses in the scene wherein Isolde selects the poison from the casket of philters which her mother had given in charge of Brangäne:

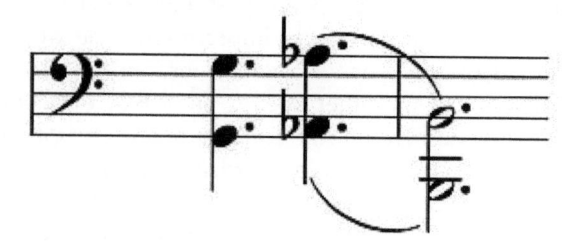

[PNG] [Listen]

There is another phrase of tragic puissance with which we must now get acquainted. At the first glance which Isolde throws upon Tristan, motionless at the helm of the ship, when the curtains are parted to permit the maid to summon the knight into the presence of the princess, this phrase publishes her dreadful determination to seek revenge for outraged love in murder and suicide. It is the symbol of death, whose relationship to the symbol of fate will easily be recognized:

Death... de - vot - ed head!

[PNG] [Listen]

Its ominous expressiveness, apart from instrumental color, which cannot be reproduced on the pianoforte, comes from the sudden and unprepared change of key from A-flat to A.

The culminating scene in the drama is that which brings the first act to a close—the meeting of Tristan and Isolde, and the drinking of the potion. In this scene the device of introducing cheerful and exciting sailors' music to heighten the intensity of a dramatic climax is used with peculiarly startling effect. It produces a marvellous illusion by the suddenness of its entrance, its sharp interruption of the tragic music expressive of the soul-torments of the principal personages, and the unprepared transition from the spectacle of doomed humanity to the joy-inspiring aspect of nature. An almost equally noteworthy effect is the orchestral proclamation of Tristan in his character as a fully-developed tragic hero. Observe how, by augmenting the simple phrase, the orchestra increases the stature of the knight; but note also how, though he looms up in Isolde's door-way like a demi-god clad in steel and brass, a knight capable of overthrowing the choicest spirits of Arthur's Round Table, and scattering thirty of King Marke's knights, the fateful harmonies in their chromatic descent (which have their model in the melody of the wounded Tristan) publish his doom with a prophetic forcefulness that cannot be misunderstood.

There is in this scene, also, a peculiarly eloquent example of the manner in which Wagner permits the music to publish hidden meanings in the text. While Brangäne, obeying her mistress's behest, is preparing the fatal draught, the gladsome noise of the sailors is heard from without. The ship is entering the harbor. Tristan, who is brooding over Isolde's demand that he drink a drink of expiation for the slaying of Morold, suddenly arouses himself. "Where are we?" he asks. "Near the goal," answers Isolde. What goal does she mean? Cornwall, the goal of the voyage? Ah, no! The music tells us; the words are sung to the death-phrase.

IV.

Wagner's skill in plunging his listeners into the mood essential to the proper reception of his drama has no brighter illustration than "Tristan und Isolde." The passionate stress and profound melancholy which mark all that really belongs to the story are prefigured for us in the prelude. That story is more than nine-tenths told in the first act. The music that is introduced to give relief to the mind, and also to heighten the tragic effect by means of contrast, is the music that is related to the scene which is the theatre of the outward action, or to the personages of the play who bear no part in the real tragedy which, as I have already intimated, plays on the stage of the lovers' hearts. These comparatively inactive persons who serve as foils are the young seaman who sings at the mast-head, the sailors, the shepherd who enters in the last act, and Kurwenal, the squire. Kurwenal, rugged yet tender, amiable and picturesque, gentle as a woman at core, shares in the bright, flowing, rhythmically vigorous music which tells of unfettered breezes, heaving billows, and popular pride; while to Tristan and Isolde is given the music made out of the few phrases which, as they unfold themselves over and over again in an infinite variety of combinations and with continually changing instrumental color, bring to our consciousness in a wonderfully vivid manner the torments which are consuming them. In the introduction to the second act we have another mood picture—a picture of the longing and impatience of the lovers; but this idea is presented with such peculiar eloquence and beauty in the first scene that I prefer to pass over the instrumental introduction with this bare reference. I am not attempting a dissection of every scene; my purpose will be attained if I can suggest the things which best indicate the mood in which it is well to listen, and give starting-points to the imagination. The second act differs from the first in that it is all but actionless. In it, however, is presented the catastrophe of the tragedy—the discovery of the guilt of the ill-starred lovers by King Marke. The scene is a garden before Queen Isolde's chamber; the time, a lovely night in summer. A torch burns in a ring beside the door leading from the chamber into the garden. The King has gone a-hunting, and as the curtain rises the tones of the hunting horns dying away in the distance blend entrancingly with an instrumental song from the orchestra, which seems a musical sublimation of night and nature in their tenderest moods. Isolde appears with Brangäne, and pleads with her to extinguish the torch and thus give a signal to Tristan, who is waiting in concealment. But Brangäne suspects treachery on the part of Melot, a knight who is jealous of Tristan and himself enamoured of Isolde, and who had planned the nocturnal hunt. She warns her mistress and begs her to wait. In their dialogue there is lovely fencing with the incident of the vanishing sounds of the hunt like Shakespeare's dalliance with nightingale and lark, in "Romeo and Juliet." Beauty rests upon this scene like a benediction. To Isolde the horns are but the rustling of the forest leaves as they are caressed by the wind, or the purling and laughing of the brook. Longing has eaten up all patience, all discretion, all fear. She extinguishes the torch in spite of Brangäne's pleadings, and with wildly waving scarf beckons on her hurrying lover. Beneath the foliage they sing their love through all the gamut of hope and despair. The text of their duet consists largely of detached ejaculations and verbal plays, each paraphrasing and varying or giving a new turn to the outpouring of the other, the whole permeated with the symbolism of pessimistic philosophy, in which night and death and oblivion (which have their symbols in the music) are glorified, and day and life (which also have their symbols) and memory are contemned. There is transporting music in the duet, and many evidences that in it Wagner wrote and composed with tremendous enthusiasm, veritably with a pen of fire. In the dialogue of this scene lies the key of the entire philosophy of the tragedy. We ought to know this, but we do not need to justify it. If I were to indulge in the unnecessary luxury of criticism, I should suggest that pessimistic philosophy transmitted through verbal plays which are carried far beyond the limits of reason, if not to the verge of childishness, is not good dramatic matter, and half an hour of it is too much. Swinburne, who repeatedly makes use of metaphors and thoughts which tempt one to believe that he made a study of Wagner's drama, also attempts a dalliance with the images of night and day which fill so many of Wagner's pages, but with a difference, and his Iseult, unlike the German Isolde, checks Tristram's song wherein he asks:

"Love, is it day that makes thee thy delight,
Or thou that seest day made out of thy light?"

by calmly observing,

"I have heard men sing of love a simpler way
Than these wrought riddles made of night and day."

I have said that we ought to know something of the philosophy of the tragedy. In Wagner's exposition of the prelude he wishes us to observe the "one glimmering of the highest bliss of attainment" in the surrender of being, the "final redemption into that wondrous realm from which we wander farthest when we try to take it by force." For this wondrous realm he chooses death and night as symbols, but what he means to imply is the Nirvana of Buddhistic philosophy, the "final deliverance of the soul from transmigration." Nirvana is the antithesis of Sansâra. Sansâra, the world, means turmoil and variety, and each new transmigration means another relapse into the miseries of existence. The love of Tristan and Isolde presents itself to Wagner as ceaseless struggle and endless contradiction, and for such a problem there is but one solution—total oblivion. Nirvana is the only conception which offers a happy outcome to such love; it means quietude and identity.

The duet is rudely interrupted in its moment of supremest ecstasy by a warning cry from Brangäne. Kurwenal dashes in with a sword and a shout: "Save thyself, Tristan!" King Marke, Melot, and courtiers at his heels. Day, the symbol of all that is fatal to their love, has dawned. Tristan is silent, though King Marke, in a long speech, bewails the treachery of his nephew and friend. Much ridicule has been poured out on this scene, which the ordinary theatre-goer finds dramatically disappointing. There can be no question that the popular sentiment is better expressed by Tennyson, in the corresponding scene in his poem, "The Last Tournament:"

"But while he bow'd to kiss the jewell'd throat,
Out of the dark, just as the lips had touch'd,
Behind him rose a shadow and a shriek—
'Mark's way,' said Mark, and clove him thro' the brain."

One need not be an advocate to say that though Marke's sermonizing may be theatrically disappointing, it offers in itself a complete defence of its propriety. From the words of the heart-torn king we learn that he had been forced into the marriage by the disturbed state of his kingdom, and that he had not consented to it until Tristan (whose purpose it was to quiet the jealous anger of the barons) had threatened to depart from Cornwall unless the King revoked his decision to make him his successor. Tristan's answer to the sorrowful upbraidings of Marke is to obtain a promise from Isolde to follow him into the "wondrous realm of Night;" then (note this as bearing on the ethics of the drama), seeing that Marke did not wield the sword of retribution, he makes a feint of attacking Melot, but permits the treacherous friend to reach him with his sword. He falls wounded unto death.

V.

The dignified, reserved knight of the first act, the impassioned lover of the second, is now a dream-haunted, longing, despairing, dying man, lying under a lime-tree in the yard of his ancestral castle in Brittany, wasting his last bit of strength in feverish fancies and ardent longings touching Isolde. Kurwenal has sent for her. Will she come? A shepherd tells of vain watches for the sight of a sail by playing a mournful melody on his pipe. What a vast expanse of empty sea is opened to our view by the ascending passages in long-drawn thirds! How vividly we are made to realize the ebbing away of Tristan's vital powers!

In the music of this act, if anywhere in the creations of Wagner, we are lifted above the necessity of seeking significances. Even the pianoforte can speak the language of this act. There is not one measure in it which does not tell its story in a manner which puts mere words to shame. Oh, the heart-hunger of the hero! The longing! Will she never come? The fever is consuming him, and his heated brain breeds fancies which one moment lift him above all memories of pain, and the next bring him to the verge of madness. Cooling breezes waft him again towards Ireland, whose princess healed the wound struck by Morold, then ripped it up again with the avenging sword with its telltale nick. From her hands he took the drink whose poison sears his heart. Accursed the cup and accursed the hand that brewed it! Will the shepherd never change his doleful strain? Ah, Isolde, how beautiful you are! The ship, the ship! It must be in sight! Kurwenal, have you no eyes? Isolde's ship! A merry tune bursts from the shepherd's pipe. It is caught up by the orchestra and whirled away on an ocean of excited sound. It is the ship! What flag flies at the peak? The flag of "All's well!" Now the ship disappears behind a cliff. There the breakers are treacherous. Who is at the helm? Friend or foe? Melot's accomplice? Are you, too, a traitor, Kurwenal?

Tristan's strength is unequal to the excitement of the moment. His mind becomes dazed. He hears Isolde's voice, and his wandering fancy transforms it into the torch whose extinction once summoned him to her side: "Do I hear the light?" He staggers to his feet and tears the bandages from his wound. "Ha, my blood, flow merrily now! She who opened the wound is here to heal it!" Life endures but for one embrace, one glance, one word—"Isolde!"—which is borne to her ears by the sadly sweet phrase, typical of the first glance of love—the word and tones which first he had uttered after the potion had made him forget all but his love.

While Isolde lies mortally stricken upon Tristan's corpse, Marke and his train arrive upon a second ship. Brangäne has told the secret of the love-draught, and the king has come to unite the lovers. But his purpose is not known, and faithful Kurwenal receives his death-blow while trying to hold the castle against Marke's men. He dies at Tristan's side. Isolde, unconscious of all these happenings, sings out her broken heart and expires.

"And ere her ear might hear, her heart had heard,
Nor sought she sign for witness of the word;
But came and stood above him, newly dead,
And felt his death upon her: and her head,
Bowed, as to reach the spring that slakes all drouth;
And their four lips became one silent mouth."

VI.

The story of Tristan and Isolde, as it was sung by the minstrel knights of the Middle Ages, is a picture of chivalry in its palmy days. We need to bear this in mind when we approach the ethical side of Wagner's version. In the music of the love duet and Isolde's death lies, perhaps, the most powerful plea ever made for the guilty lovers. No one will stray far from the judgment which the future will pronounce on Wagner's creations, I imagine, who sets down Isolde's swan's song as the choicest flower of Wagner's creative faculty, the culmination of his powers as a composer. I do not believe that the purifying and ennobling capacity of music was ever before or since demonstrated as it is here. While listening to this tonal beatification, it is difficult to hear the voice of reason pronouncing the judgment of outraged law. Yet it is right that that voice should be heard. It is due to the poet-composer that it should be heard. Wagner's attitude towards the old legend differs vastly from that of the poets who preceded him in treating it.

In the days of chivalry depicted by Gottfried von Strassburg and the other mediæval poets who have sung the passion of these lovers, the odor which assails our moral sense as the odor of death and decay was esteemed the sweetest incense that arose from a poet's censer. Read the *Wachtlieder* of the German *Minnesinger*. The German *Wachtlied*, the Provençal *alba*, is the song sung by the squire or friend watching without, warning the lovers to separate. Brangäne's song in the second act is such a *Wachtlied*. Read the decisions of the Courts of Love, which governed the actions of chivalrous knighthood when chivalry was at its zenith. Again and again was it proclaimed by these tribunals that conjugal duty shut out the possibility of love between husband and wife. In the economy of feudal castle life there was no provision for women. The place was the domicile of warriors. Daughters of the lord of the castle were married off in childhood. Who, then, could be the object of knightly love? The answer is not far to seek. The service of woman to which mediæval knighthood was devoted, the service which is celebrated in words which we can scarcely accept, except as wildest hyperbole, was the service paid to another man's wife. And the fact that the knight himself had a wife was not a hinderance but an incentive to the service which was the occupation of his life. Now think for a moment on Wagner's modification of the Tristram legend. From it he eliminates the second Iseult. His hero cannot contract a loveless marriage, and at one stroke one element in the attitude of the sexes which appears strange, unnatural, and shocking to us, is wiped from the story.

The versions of Gottfried von Strassburg, Matthew Arnold, Swinburne, Tennyson, and Wagner present three points of view from which the love of the tragic pair must be studied. With the first three the drinking is purely accidental, and the passion which leads to the destruction of the lovers is something for which they are in no wise responsible. With Tennyson there is no philter, and the passion is all guilty. With Wagner the love exists before the dreadful drinking, and the potion is less a maker of uncontrollable passion than a drink which causes the lovers to forget duty, honor, and the respect due to the laws of society. It is a favorite idea of Wagner's that the hero of tragedy should be a type of humanity freed from all the bonds of conventionality. It is unquestionable in my mind that in his scheme we are to accept the love-potion as merely the agency with which Wagner struck from his hero the shackles of convention.

Unquestionably, as Bayard Taylor argued, the love-draught is the Fate of the Tristan drama, and this brings into notice the significance of Wagner's chief variation. It is an old theory, too often overlooked now, that there must be at least a taint of guilt in the conduct of a tragic hero in order that the feeling of pity excited by his sufferings may not overcome the idea of justice in the catastrophe. This theory was plainly an outgrowth of the deep religious purpose of the Greek tragedy. Wagner puts antecedent and conscious guilt at the door of both his heroic characters. They love before the philter, and do not pay the reverence to the passion which, in the highest conception, it commands. Tristan is carried away by love of power and glory before men, and himself suggests and compels by his threats

Marke's marriage, which is a crime against the love which he bears Isolde and she bears him. There is guilt enough in Isolde's determination and effort to commit murder and suicide. Thus Wagner presents us the idea of Fate in the latest and highest aspect that it assumed in the minds of the Greek poets, and he arouses our pity and our horror, not only by the sufferings of the principals, but also by making an innocent and amiable prompting to underlie the action which brings down the catastrophe. It is Brangäne's love for her mistress that persuades her to shield her from the crime of murder and protect her life. From whatever point of view the question is treated, it seems to me that Wagner's variation is an improvement on the old legend, and that the objection, which German critics have urged, that the love of the pair is merely a chemical product, and so, outside of human sympathy, falls to the ground.

CHAPTER III.
"DIE MEISTERSINGER VON NÜRNBERG."

Once upon a time—if I were disposed to be circumstantial I would say in the early summer of the year of our Lord 1560, for it was the year of Hans Sachs' widowerhood—Veit Pogner, desiring to honor the craft of the master-singers in Nuremberg, to whose guild he belonged, offered a rare prize as the reward of the victor in a singing contest to be held on St. John's Day. Pogner was a rich silversmith who had travelled much, who had loved the arts of song and song-making, and whose pride had been hurt by the discovery that the gentry and nobility of the German nation affected to despise the humble burgher for his too great devotion to money-getting, unmindful of the fact, which Pogner knew full well, that what there was of art-love and devotion and talent was possessed and encouraged by the common people. It was for this reason that he resolved to stimulate a supreme effort in the form of art which most interested him, and the prize which he offered was nothing less than his only child Eva in marriage, with all his great wealth as a dowry. But Eva, dutiful in the main if rather forward and self-willed, was little inclined to be bestowed as a prize unless she had the picking of the winner. The fact is, she had lost her heart to a handsome young knight from Franconia—in the course of a flirtation carried on during divine service, I regret to say—and had told him so in a somewhat impetuous manner, scarcely consistent with modern notions on the subject of young women's behavior. She had not thought it necessary to take her father into her confidence, and so the young Franconian knight, who had come to Nuremberg to repair his fortunes, was reduced to the extremity of entering the Guild of master-singers, so that he might be qualified to go into the competition on the morrow. A trial of candidates for admission to the guild had been announced for that very day after divine service, and Walther von Stolzing (that was the young knight's name) entered the lists. But, alas! he knew nothing of the code of laws which governed the structure of master-songs and prescribed the thirty-two offences which must not be committed. Nor did he count on the fact that the adjudicator who would keep tally of his violations of those laws would be Sixtus Beckmesser, the town-clerk, whose longing glances were also turned in Eva's direction—or, at least, towards her father's gold. He went into the contest trusting to the inspiration of his love and his memory of the spirit which breathes through the songs of that ardent old nature-lover, Walther von der Vogelweide, whom the master-singers counted among the founders of their guild, to carry him through. When the time came for him to improvise a song which was to determine whether or not he was fit to be a master-singer, he sang: now pouring out an ecstasy of feeling, and anon scorching with scornful allusions the jealous pedant behind the judge's curtain. In a burst of enthusiasm he rose from the chair in which the code required the singer to sit, and this completed his discomfiture. Hans Sachs, who, as he used to say, was "shoemaker and poet, too," indeed had recognized evidences of genius in the song, and its newness of style and indifference to ancient formula seemed to him to weigh little as against its freshness and eloquence and ardor. But Sachs could not prevent judgment going against the singer. That night the young couple resolved to elope and seek their happiness outside the code of laws of the Master-singers, but were interrupted by the circumstance that Sachs, haunted by the song of the knight whose cause he had espoused, was unable to sleep, and had resolved to finish a pair of shoes ordered by Beckmesser. Sachs was kindly disposed towards the lovers, but he had a strong sense of the duty due to parents. He saw the pair in the shadow of a tree while he was musing on the occurrences of the day, and suspected their purpose, as, indeed, he well might, for Eva had changed her head-dress for that of her maid, Magdalena. As if without special purpose, he drew his bench to the door, and threw a ray of light across the street, through which they would be obliged to pass. In another moment the malicious town-clerk appeared on the scene with a lute. He had come to serenade Eva, in the hope of making an impression which would be useful to him on the morrow, for it had been stipulated that though the winner of the prize must be a master-singer, yet Eva was to have a voice in the decision. While Magdalena took her place at the window to delude Beckmesser with the belief that his serenade was being listened to by its object, Sachs interrupted the malicious clown by lustily shouting a song as he cobbled at the bench, pleading in extenuation, when Beckmesser remonstrated with him, that he must finish the shoes, for want of which Beckmesser had twitted him at the meeting in St. Catherine's Church a few hours before. Finally, having reduced the boor to the verge of distraction, Sachs agreed to listen to his serenade, provided he were allowed the privilege of playing adjudicator and marking the errors of composition by striking his lapstone. The errors were not few, and, as you may imagine, each critical tap threw Beckmesser into more of a rage, until he lost his head altogether, and Sachs beat such a tattoo on his lapstone that he had finished his work when Beckmesser came to the end of his song, which, we may believe, was comical enough. And now, to complete Beckmesser's misery, David, an apprentice of Sachs' and Magdalena's sweetheart, thinking that the serenade had been intended for her, began to belabor the singer with a club; the hubbub called the neighbors into the street, and, as many of them bore little grudges against each other, they took occasion to feed them all fat. A right merry brawl was in progress when the watchman's horn was heard. Quick as a flash the brawlers disappeared, and when the sleepy old watchman entered the street none of the peace disturbers was to be seen; the old Dogberry stared about him in amazement, rubbed his eyes, sang the monotonous chant which told the hour and cautioned the burghers against spooks, and walked off in the peaceful moonlight.

Next morning Walther, who had been taken in by Sachs, sang the recital of a dream which had enriched his sleep. It was as beautiful in the telling as in the experience, and Sachs transcribed it, punctuating the pauses with bits of advice which enabled Walther easily to throw it into the form of a master-song which would pass the muster even of the pedantic code, though a few liberties were taken in the matter of melody. While Sachs was absent from his shop to don clothes meet for the coming festivities, Beckmesser came in and found the song, which he conveyed to his own pocket. Sachs, returning, discovered the theft, and gave the song to the thief, who, knowing Sachs' great talent in composition, secured a promise from him not to claim it as his own, and to permit him to sing it at the contest. This suited Sachs' purposes admirably. A few hours later all the good people of Nuremberg were gathered on the meadow just outside the walls, which was their customary place of merrymaking. The guilds were there—the cobblers and tailors and bakers and toy-makers—God bless 'em!—with trumpeters and drummers and pipers, and hundreds of spruce apprentices; and the master-singers with their banner and insignia, headed by Sachs. Beckmesser was there, too, with the words of Walther's song whirling in a hopeless maze in his addled pate. He tried to sing it, but made a monstrously stupid parody, and when the populace hooted and railed and jeered at him for presuming to aspire to the hand of the beauteous Eva he flew into a rage, charged the authorship of the song which had caused his downfall on Sachs, and left the field to his rival Walther, who, to vindicate Sachs' statement that the song was a good one when well sung, presently burdened the air with its loveliness, adding, in his enthusiasm, an improvised apostrophe to Eva and the Parnassus of poetry. Master-singers, people—and Eva—were agreed that the gallant knight had won the prize, and Sachs gently compelled him, in spite of his protest, to take the master-singer's medallion along with the bride, and charged him never more to affect to despise the German masters of song, whose works shall live though the Holy Roman Empire go up in smoke.

I.

The story of "Die Meistersinger von Nürnberg" furnishes more food for reflection than one might think at first blush, and opens a channel of thought not commonly used when Wagner is in mind. It is a comedy, and it is easiest to think of Wagner as a tragedian. Yet it is not the smallest of his achievements that, more thoroughly and consistently than any dramatist of our time, he has in his works restored the boundary line which in the classic world separated comedy from tragedy. In "Tannhäuser," "Tristan und Isolde," and "The Niblung's Ring" are found examples of the old tragedy type. They deal with grand passions, and their heroes are gods or god-like men who are shattered against Fate. His only essay in the field of comedy was made in "Die Meistersinger," and this is as faithful to the old conception of comedy as the other dramas are to the classic ideals of tragedy. It deals with the manners and follies and vices of the common people, and exemplifies the purpose of comedy as it was set down in one of the truest and best definitions ever written. It aims to chastise manners with a smile. There are two ways of looking at "Die Meistersinger." It can be weighted with a symbolical character, or it can be taken as an example of pure comedy, with no deeper significance than lies on the easily-reached surface of its lines, action, and music. There is no doubt that Wagner conceived it as a satire, and it is even possible (although I can recall no direct statement of his to that effect) that he intended to chastise with it the spirit of conservatism and pedantry which was for so long a time a stumbling-block in the way of his system. Telling of his first draft of the comedy in 1845, immediately after the completion of "Tannhäuser," he said that he had planned it as a satyr-play after the tragedy, and, conceiving Hans Sachs as the last example of the artistically productive Folk-spirit, had placed him in opposition to the master-singer burgherdom, to whose droll and rule-of-thumb pedantry he gave individual expression in the character of the adjudicator, or *Merker*. This statement, although it was made nearly a generation before the comedy was written, justifies the assumption that it was his purpose in it to celebrate the triumph of the natural poetic impulse, stimulated by communion with nature, over pedantic formulas. But a word of caution should be uttered against the autobiographic stamp which some extremists have wanted to impress upon it. The comedy is not rendered more interesting or its satire more admirable by thinking of Walther as the prototype of Wagner himself, of Beckmesser as Wagner's opponents, and of Hans Sachs as King Ludwig, embodying in himself, furthermore, the symbol of enlightened public opinion, which neither despises rules nor is willing to be ridden by them. Such an exposition of its symbolism lies near enough in its broad lines, but there is danger in carrying it through all the details of the plot. When it is too far pushed, critics will ask in the future, as they have asked in the past, how this can be accepted as the satirical motive of the comedy when the hero who triumphs over the supposed evil principle in the drama does so, not to advance the virtue which stands in opposition to that evil principle, but simply to win a bride—a purpose that is purely selfish, however amiable and commendable it may be. Walther does, indeed, discover himself as the champion of spontaneous, vital art, and the antagonist of the pedantry represented by the master-singers; but this is not until after he has learned that he can only win the young lady by himself becoming a member of the guild, and defeating all comers at the tournament of song. Knowing none of the rules, he boldly relies on the potency of the inspiration begotten by his love, and does his best under the circumstances; that he ultimately succeeds he owes to the help of Sachs, and the fact that his rival defeats himself by resorting to foul means. Besides, to justify fully this dramatic scheme, Beckmesser ought not to have been made the blundering idiot and foolish knave that he appears to be in the stage versions, but at the worst a short-sighted, narrow-minded, and perhaps malicious pedant. As he stands in the stage representations Beckmesser is an ill-natured and wicked buffoon, a caricature of a peculiarly gross kind, and only an infinitesimally tiny corrective idea lies in the fact that a manly young knight who loves a pretty young woman should have saved her from falling into such a rival's hands by marrying her himself. He would have had the vote of the public on his side if he had sung like a crow and Beckmesser like Anacreon.

II.

If we will look upon the contest symbolized in the comedy, not as that between Wagner and his contemporaries, but as between the two elements in art whose opposition stimulates life, and whose union, perfect, peaceful, mutually supplemental, is found in every really great art-work, I think we shall come pretty near the truth. At least, we will have an interesting point of view from which to study its musical and literary structure. Simply for convenience sake let us call these two principles Romanticism and Classicism. The terms are a little vague, entirely arbitrary, and if we were seeking scientific exactness we should be obliged to condemn their use. Popularly, they are conceived as antithetical in the critical history of literature as well as music. It is in this sense (with a difference) that I wish to use them.

If the history of music be looked at with a view to discovering the spirit which animates its products rather than observing their integument, it will be found that from the beginning two forces have been in operation, and by their antagonism have done the work of progressive creation. In the religious chant, with its restrictive clog (the fruit of superstitious veneration and fear) we find that manifestation of the spirit of antique music which was chiefly instrumental in its establishment and regulation. To that spirit tribute above its meed is paid in the hand-books which begin the history of modern music with the chants of the Christian Church. The other spirit, having been cultivated outside the church, has had fewer historians to do it reverence. It is the free, untrammelled impulse which rests on the law of nature and refuses the domination of formal rule and restrictive principle.

On the love-song, war-song, and hunting-song of early man, on the cradle-song crooned by early woman, there rested not the weight of superstitious fear and hope which fettered the religious chant. They were individual manifestations of feeling, and in them the fancy was free to discover and use all the tonal and rhythmical combinations which might be helpful in giving voice to emotion. The mission of this spirit (which I will call Romanticism to distinguish it from the conservative, and regulative spirit which I will call Classicism) was fulfilled, during the artificiality and all-pervading scholasticism of the Middle Ages, by the *Minnesinger* and *trouvère*; and though the death of chivalry ended that peculiar ministry, the spirit continued to live as it had lived from the beginning, as it still lives and will live *in sæcula sæculorum*, in the people's songs and dances. When the composers of two hundred and fifty years ago began to develop instrumental music they found the germ of the sonata form—the form that made Beethoven's symphonies possible—in the homely dance tunes of the people which till then had been looked upon as vulgar things, wholly outside the domain of polite art. The genius of the masters of the last century moulded this form of plebeian ancestry into a vessel of wonderful beauty; but by the time this had been done the capacity of music as an emotional language had been greatly increased, and the same Romantic spirit which had originally created the dance forms that they might embody the artistic impulses of that early time, suggested the filling of the vessel with the new contents. When the vessel would not hold these new contents it had to be widened. New bottles for new wine. That is the whole mystery of what conservative critics decry as the destruction of form in music. It is not destruction, but change. When you destroy form you destroy music, for the musical essence can manifest itself only through form.

As a perfectly natural result of the development of this beautiful and efficient vessel called the Sonata form, a love of symmetry and order, of correct logic and beautiful sequence, came to dominate composers, and it is a relic of this love, a love which we must not despise in such masters as Haydn and Mozart, which led them to fill so many of their compositions with repetitions of parts and conventional passages that appear meaningless and wearisome to us. They were written in compliance with the demands of form.

III.

For the purposes of our exposition of the symbolism of Wagner's comedy, of the meaning of its satire, we shall have to look upon classical composers as those who developed music chiefly on its formal side and conserved the laws which enabled them to reach one ideal of beauty. The Romantic composers will then be those who sought their ideals in other regions than the formal, and strove to give them expression irrespective—or, if necessary, in defiance—of the conventions of law. Romanticism will appear to us as the creative principle, and hence we shall find it in Wagner's comedy associated with Youth, its passions and enthusiasms; with Love, and heedless, reckless daring; with Spring and blooming time; with the singing of birds and the perfume of flowers; with assertion of the right of unfettered utterance and denial of the wisdom or justice of reflection and moderation.

Do not visions corresponding with these attributes rise up out of the incidents of the play? The lovers, with their impetuous love-making and reckless resolve which sapient Sachs frustrates; Walther's songs in the first act, telling of Spring releasing Nature from her icy shackles and winning her smiles, while sunlight and birds and meadow flowers, and the old poet who sang the praises of them and was named after the mead he loved, united in teaching him the art of song; the bold defiance of the master-singers and their code; the rejection of the medal when it had been won. Classicism, in turn, will appear as the regulative and conservative principle, and its association in the play will be with maturity of age and moderation in thought and action; with personages in whom the creative impulse is not an elemental force, but a pleasure or a duty which waits upon the judgment; also, for satirical purposes, with a guild of handicraftsmen and tradespeople who enforce an apprenticeship in art as they do in trade; who think that by adherence to rule artworks may be created as shoes are made over a last; who are pompous in their pedantry and amiable only in the holy simplicity of their earnestness, their vanity, and their complacency. Such are the associations which arise when the pictures of the comedy are passed in hasty review; and they have been grievously incomplete. They have omitted the real hero of the play, the poet who belongs to the guild and upholds its laws while battling for the spirit represented by him who falls under the condemnation of those very laws. Where is Hans Sachs? Search him out. You will find him in the midst of the combatants fighting valiantly *on both sides*; representing a principle at once creative and conservative, standing, in the history of artistic development, for those true geniuses who breathe the breath of life into the body, not for the purpose of destruction, but that the spirit may become manifest in the flesh.

It is contest which brings life. All the great classical composers from Brahms back to Bach have had their moments of Romantic feeling; it is never absent from the truly creative artist; but its most eloquent expression was reserved for our century. You recognize it in the whole body of instrumental music, beginning with Beethoven; you yield to its influence when you hear the operas of Gluck, Mozart, and Weber. The musicians whose influence was strongest when Wagner began his reforms were frank in their protestations of allegiance to this conception of Romanticism: "The Spirit builds the forms, or finds them ready-built, and refashions them according to its needs and desires," said Marx. "If you wish to adopt art as a profession you cannot accustom yourself early enough to consider the contents of an art-work as more important and serious a matter than its structure," said Mendelssohn, the greatest master of form that the century has known. "That would be a trivial art which would have only sounds but no language or signs for the conditions of the soul," said Schumann.

Wagner was too thorough an artist, too profound a musician, not to recognize the value of constructive law. He would have been false to his principles and false to his practice had he written a comedy for the purpose of glorifying mere lawlessness. Had this been his purpose he would not have told us as he has that it was Sachs whom he intended to oppose to the spirit of pedantry and formalism personified in Beckmesser. Sachs has no condemnation to pronounce on the laws of the guild of which he was the brightest ornament. On the contrary, he upholds them even against Walther, and persuades him to adopt them in the composition of his prize song, just as after the victory is won he admonishes him to give the reverence due to the masters. What he learns from Walther, and impresses on his colleagues, is the need of adapting form to spirit, and the mental conflict which brings him to this conviction is a reflection of that creative activity which looks to the short-sighted like destructive war, but is exemplified in the works of the great masters as the highest peace. We can gain an insight into the musical structure of the comedy, and find proofs for our contention at the same time, if we observe Sachs under the influence of this seeming contradiction.

It is evening, and the poet has returned to his cobbler's bench. The scent of the elder-tree, the charm of the summer night, will not permit him to work; they turn his thoughts to poetry; but memories of Walther's song come over him, and under their influence he can neither work nor compose. There was an inexplicable charm in the song. No rule would fit it, yet it was faultless. It was new and strange, yet sounded old and familiar, like the carolling of birds in May-time. To try to imitate it would result in shame and contumely. That he knew. Where lay the mystery? At last he discovers it. The song was the voice of Spring, of the heyday of the singer's life and passion. The need of utterance brought with it the capacity and the privilege. All this we may learn from the words of Sachs, while the music tells us of what is passing through his mind in the intervals of his soliloquizing. This music is built up out of a very short phrase, but it is the phrase which may be set down as the chief musical symbol of the spirit which I have called Romanticism:

[PNG] [Listen]

To learn why this phrase should haunt the mind of Sachs its genesis must be traced. It is found first to enter the score of the drama (after the prelude) to accompany a tender but urgent glance of inquiry which Walther bestows on Eva in the first scene between the lines of the *chorale* sung by the congregation:

[PNG] [Listen]

Next, when Eva shyly rebukes his ardor with a glance, but quickly returns it with emotion:

[PNG] [Listen]

When the congregation breaks up, Walther, gazing intently on Eva, from whom he had received a look which confessed her love (accompanied by a phrase which afterwards plays an important role in his prize song), hurries to address her; his eagerness is published by the orchestra in this variation of the phrase:

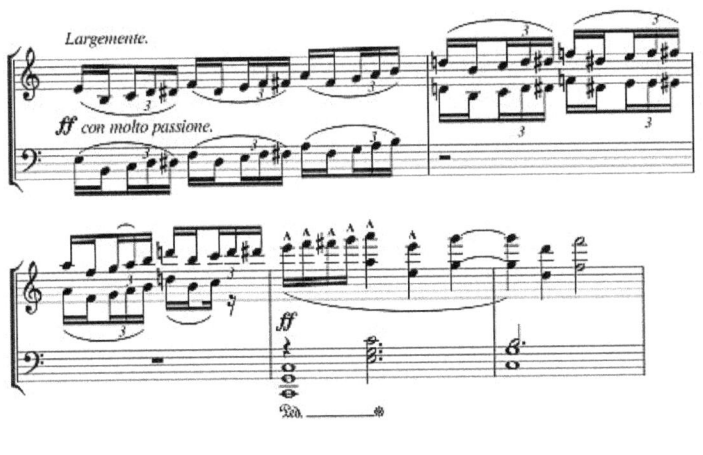

[PNG] [Listen]

A threefold augmentation of the phrase is shown in these examples, which suffice to identify it with one of the fundamental feelings concerned in the play. It depicts or typifies the youthful impetuosity of the lovers, the ardor of their passion before it had been confessed in words. Is not its fitness for such a mission obvious? Observe the eagerness which the triplet injects into its rhythm, the ebulliency expressed by the tendency of its melody to ascend ever higher and higher in the regions of tonality. Poetical association consorts analogous attributes with Love and Youth and Spring-time; and it is in the song which Walther sings in praise of Spring and Love—his trial song in the first act—that the phrase receives its most eloquent treatment. Note the irrepressible enthusiasm of its proclamation in this song (*Fanget an!*); how, after a peaceful announcement, it surges upward and ever upward in the accompaniment, until the voice can no longer hold out against but is borne up on it, until left by a scintillant explosion which seems to be the only means at hand to bring the jubilant phrase back into control. This is the Romantic expression which haunted the mind of Sachs when, after the stormy meeting in St. Catherine's Church, he thought to work in the perfumed quiet of the evening.

IV.

In broad lines the prelude to "Die Meistersinger" not only serves to delineate the characteristic traits of the personages concerned in the comedy, but also exhibits Wagner's method of musical exposition, and teaches the lesson which is at the bottom of the satire—the lesson, namely, that it is through the union of the two principles, which until the close of the play appear in conflict, that a genuine work of art is quickened. The prelude contains the whole symbolism of the comedy in a nutshell. In form it is unique, but in so far as it employs only melodies drawn from the play it may not incorrectly be classed with the medley overtures which composers used to throw together for ante-curtain music. It is the manner in which Wagner has treated his melodies, and the delineative capacity with which he has endowed them, that render the prelude a capital exemplification of the theory advanced by Gluck, when, in his preface to "Alceste," he said, "I imagined that the overture ought to prepare the audience for the action of the piece, and serve as a kind of argument to it." Wagner follows this precept and the example set by Beethoven in the "Leonore" overtures, and indicates the elements of the plot, their progress in its development, and finally the outcome, in his symphonic introduction. The melodies which are its constructive material are of two classes, broadly distinguished in external physiognomy and emotional essence. They are presented first consecutively, then as in conflict (first one, then another, pushing forward for expression), finally in harmonious and contented union. It should always be borne in mind that no matter how numerous the hand-books—which a witty German critic called "musical Baedeckers"—if one wishes to know Wagner's purpose in the use of a typical phrase or melody, he need take no one's word for it except Wagner's. He can turn to the score and trace it out himself, learning its meaning from the words and situations with which it is associated. If this plan be followed, it will be seen that the master-singers are throughout the comedy characterized by two melodies,

[PNG] [Listen]

and

[PNG] [Listen]

Note that as the master-singers belonged to the solid burghers of old Nuremberg—a little vain, as was to be expected in the upholders of an institution of great antiquity and glorious traditions; staid, dignified, and complacent, as became the free citizens of a free imperial city, whose stout walls sheltered the best in art and science that Germany could boast—so these two melodies are strong, simple tunes; sequences of the intervals of the simple diatonic scale; strongly and simply harmonized; square-cut in rhythm; firm and dignified, if a trifle pompous, in their stride. The three melodies belonging to the class presented in opposition to the spirit represented by the master-singers are disclosed by a study of the comedy to be associated with the passion of the young lovers, Walther and Eva, and those influences in nature which are the inspiration of romantic utterance—spring-time, the birds, and flowers. They differ in every respect—melodic, rhythmic, harmonic, as well as in treatment—from the melodies which stand for the old master-singers and their notions. They are chromatic; their rhythms are less regular and more eager (through the agency of syncopation); they are harmonized with greater warmth, and set for the instruments with greater passion. The first,

[PNG] [Listen]

most surely tells us of the incipiency of the lovers' passion, for it is the subject of the interludes between the lines of the *chorale* which accompany the flirtation in the church scene. The second,

[PNG] [Listen]

is again concerned with the passion, showing it in the phase of ardent longing. Another is the melody to which Walther sings the last stanza of his prize song. I have already quoted and described it as the phrase to which Eva confesses her love by a gesture of the eyes in the church scene. Lest the significance of that telltale glance should not be recognized, observe that both lovers use the melody in their protestations of devotion to each other at parting:

[PNG] [Listen]

The fourth is the impatiently aspiring phrase described in the analysis of Sachs' monologue.

There is another theme which is of less importance, seemingly, in the score, but which plays a happy part in the comedy as it is prefigured in the prelude. It is the rhythmically strongly-marked phrase with which the populace jeers at Beckmesser, and effects his discomfiture in the final scene of the play.

[PNG] [Listen]

This little phrase it is which performs the duty of musical satirist in the middle part of the prelude, where the grotesque elements in the character of Beckmesser are pictured. It is a *scherzando* movement, the master-singers' march melody being presented in diminution by the choir of wood-wind instruments, which persist stubbornly in their fussy cackling, in spite of the fact that the strings take every opportunity to send some of the passionate, pushing, pulsating love music surging through the desiccated mass of tones.

Here it is that Wagner chastises the foolish manners of the master-singers, as he does later in the actual representation. The jeering phrase, started by the middle strings, eventually cuts through the mass of tones, and when the caricature of the broad melody, typical of the master-singers, has been laughed out of court, the music which exemplifies the freshness and vigor of Youth and Spring and Love, and their right to free and spontaneous proclamation, masters the orchestra and conquers recognition, and even celebration, from the representatives of conservatism and pedantry. In the musical contest it is only the perverted idea of Classicism which is treated with contumely and routed; the glorification of the triumph of Romanticism is found in the stupendously pompous and brilliant setting given to the master-singers' music at the end.

You see already in this prelude that Wagner is a true comedian. He administers chastisement with a smile (*ridendo castigat mores*), and chooses for its subject only things which are temporary aberrations from the good. What is strong and true and pure and wholesome in the art of the master-singers he permits to pass through his satirical fires unscathed. Classicism in its original sense, as the conservator of that which is highest and best in art, he leaves unharmed, presenting her after her trial, as Tennyson presents his Princess, at the close of his corrective poem, when

"All
Her falser self slipt from her like a robe,
And left her woman, lovelier in her mood
Than in her mould that other, when she came
From barren deeps to conquer all with love."

V.

The third act of the comedy is preceded by a prelude which, rightly understood, reflects the cobbler-poet whom I have chosen to think the real hero of the play, in the light in which he appears in the history of German civilization and culture. Twice before, in the comedy, a glimpse of him in that character had been given—in the summer evening, after the meeting, when he could not work because he was haunted by the memory of Walther's song, and again when, having found the solution of the problem raised by that song, he drove away all the phantoms of melancholy by his lusty cobbling song. Apparently that song is all carelessness and contentment, but in reality it tells of the lofty thinker and his melancholy, bred of his contemplation of the vanities of the things with which he finds himself surrounded.

This is the last stanza:

"O Eve, my sore complaints attend,
My needs and dire distresses,
For underfoot mankind the cobbler's work of art oppresses.
If I'd no angel knew
What 'tis to make a shoe,
I'd leave this cobbling in a trice.
But when I go to his retreat,
I leave the world beneath my feet,
Myself I view, Hans Sachs a shoemaker and song-master too!"

In the accompaniment to this stanza a phrase appears in the orchestra (it is not in the simplified pianoforte scores) in which, as Wagner himself puts it, there is "the bitter cry of resignation of the man who shows to the world a cheerful and energetic mien." It is the solemn phrase which gives character and color to Sachs' monologue in the third act, when he contemplates the follies and petty passions of humanity (*Wahn! Wahn! überall Wahn!*). It symbolizes for us Sachs, the philosopher. To appreciate the full significance of the Nuremberg cobbler as poet and thinker, a glance must be thrown upon a highly important phase in the history of German culture. A new melody had been put into that voice by the Reformation. Luther lived to be hailed by it as "the Nightingale of Wittenberg" in a poem whose opening lines Wagner ingeniously uses as a tribute to Sachs in the third act of the comedy. It is the chorale, *Wach auf! Es nahet gen dem Tag.*

The Reformation had revived interest in the old art of master-song which had sunk into decadence under the edict of the Romish Church prohibiting the reading of the Bible by the common people. The greatest of the Nuremberg school of master-singers was inspired by the new dawn, and Luther and Melanchthon looked up from the pages of Homer, Virgil, and Horace to listen to the strange new melody which felt and sang with and for the people. This character of Sachs, in all the details that I have pointed out, is delineated in the prelude to the third act, whose melodic contents are thus summarized: First, the contemplative phrase, *Wahn! Wahn!* next the Lutheran chorale, *Wach auf!* a portion of the cobbling song ("as if the man had turned his gaze from his handiwork heavenwards, and was lost in tender musing," says Wagner); then the chorale again, with increased sonority, and eventually the opening phrase attuned to cheerfulness and resignation.

VI.

Wagner's "Meistersinger von Nürnberg" is a comedy, and by that token is more difficult of understanding and appreciation by persons unfamiliar with the German tongue, history, and social customs than any of his tragedies. In considering the latter, it is only the elements of expression that need give us pause. In their essence, being true tragedies, they are as much the property of one race as another. This is not the case with comedies. They do not deal with the great fundamental passions of humanity, but with the petty foibles and follies and vices of a people. Being such, they vary with peoples and with times, and their representation compels the use of historical backgrounds, the application of local color. "Die Meistersinger" is a capital illustration of this principle of dramatic poetry. As a picture of the social life of a German city three hundred years ago its vividness and truthfulness are beyond praise; it has no equal in operatic literature, and few peers in the literature of the spoken drama. It is absolutely photographic in its accuracy. To appreciate this fact fully one must have visited Nuremberg, gone through its museum, and turned over the records. With such assistance it is easy to call up in fancy such a vision of its social life in the middle of the sixteenth century as will form a most harmonious setting for the series of pictures which Wagner created. It is still the quaintest city in Germany, and full of relics of its old glory. Of these relics, however, fewer belong to the time of the master-singers than an investigator would be likely to imagine. In the Germanic Museum may be found remains of many of the old guilds of the town, but none of the Master-singers' Guild, except a tablet which once hung on the walls of St. Catherine's Church and has been removed to the museum for safe-keeping. The church, indeed, is still in existence, but its use by the master-singers never brought it fame until after Wagner's comic opera had been written, and now I doubt whether a hundred residents of Nuremberg, aside from those who live in the immediate vicinity, could even tell a visitor where to find it. For more than a century it has been put to secular uses, and nothing of the interior remains to indicate what it looked like in the time of Hans Sachs except the walls. All the furniture and decorations were long ago removed, for it has been a painters' academy, drawing-school, military hospital, warehouse, public hall, and perhaps a dozen other things since it ceased to be a place of public worship. Just now it is the paint-shop of the Municipal Theatre. It is a small, unpretentious building, absolutely innocent of architectural beauty, hidden away in the middle of a block of lowly buildings used as dwellings, carpenter-shops, and the like. I got the keys from a sort of police supervisor of the district and inspected the interior in 1886. The janitor knew nothing about its history beyond his own memory, and that compassed only a portion of its career as a sort of municipal lumber-room. It was built in the last half-decade of the thirteenth century, and on its water-stained walls can be seen faint bits of the frescos which once adorned it and were painted in the fourteenth, fifteenth, and sixteenth centuries; but they are ruined beyond recognition or hope of restoration. I went to the director of the Germanic Museum to learn what had become of the old church furniture. He did not know.

"Have you seen the tablet of the master-singers which we have up-stairs?" he asked.

"Yes."

"Well, that is all that we have in the way of master-singer relics. If you have seen that and the church, you have seen all, and will have to compose the rest of the picture—draw on your imagination, or hire an artist to do it for you."

The tablet is really a more interesting relic than the church. It is a small affair of wood, with two doors, and was painted by a Franz Hein in 1581. On the doors are portraits of four distinguished members of the guild. Two pictures occupy the middle panel, the upper, with a charmingly naïve disregard of chronology, showing King David praying before a crucifix; the lower, a meeting of master-singers with a singer perched in a box-like pulpit. Over the heads of the assemblage is a representation of the chain and medallion with which the victor in a singing contest used to be decorated. Sachs gave one of these ornaments to the guild, and it was used for a hundred years. By that time, however, it had become so worn that Johann Christoph Wagenseil, a professor of Oriental languages at the University of Altdorf (to whose book, entitled *De Sacri Rom. Imperii Libera Civitate Noribergensi Commentatio*, printed in 1697, we owe the greater part of our knowledge of the art and customs of the *Meistersinger*), replaced it with another. The tablet might offer suggestions to the theatrical costumer touching the dress of the master-singers, and also the picture of David and his harp which ornamented their banner; but old Nuremberg costumes are familiar enough, and can be studied to better purpose elsewhere. Only one feature suggests itself as worthy of special notice. On the tablet the master-singers all appear wearing the immense neck-ruff of the Elizabethan period. As for the architectural settings of the stage in the first act (which plays in the Church of St. Catherine), so far as I know no attempt at correctness has been made by scene-painters; nor would it be possible to reproduce a picture of the church and still follow Wagner's stage directions. Evidently the poet-composer never took the trouble to visit the Church of St. Catherine.

WOODEN TABLET OF THE MASTERSINGERS OF NUREMBERG.

I have said that, barring the church and tablet, there are no relics of the old guild to be found in the Nuremberg of to-day. Until lately it was supposed that the Municipal Library contained a number of autographic manuscripts by Hans Sachs, but when I asked for them, they were produced with the statement that they were no longer looked upon as genuine. It did not require much investigation to convince me that the claim long maintained that they were autographs of the cobbler-poet rested wholly on presumption. Sachs autographs are extremely scarce. The Royal Library at Berlin possesses a volume of master-songs known to be in the handwriting of Sachs (among them is one by Beckmesser), but when I was in the Prussian capital this treasure was in Dresden, whither it had been sent to enable a literary student to utilize it in the preparation of a book on Sachs. A Berlin scholar, whom I found at work in the Nuremberg Library gathering material for a new biography of Sachs, informed me that the greatest number of Sachs autographs, and they not many, had been found in Zwickau, whither they had been brought by some member of the Sachs family many years ago. There are, then, no manuscript relics of him who was the chief glory of the Nuremberg guild in the old town. You may drink a glass of wine at the street-corner where tradition says the old poet cobbled and composed, but the house is a modern one. Of his companions in the guild I found no manuscripts in the library, and not one of them left his mark in any way on the town. But I did find a number of old manuscript volumes dating back two hundred years or more, which served to vitalize in a peculiarly interesting manner the record which the learned old Wagenseil left behind him, and some of the personages of Wagner's comedy. Those who have taken the trouble to investigate the source to which Wagner went for the people and customs introduced in his "Meistersinger von Nürnberg" (Wagenseil's book) know that the names of the master-singers who figure in the comedy once belonged to veritable members of the Nuremberg guild. Wagenseil mentions them as singers whose memories were cherished in his day, and some of them were also mentioned by an older author, whose book, devoted chiefly to the Strassburg guild, which at one time was even more famous than that of Nuremberg, is referred to by Wagenseil. The book of the Strassburg writer, singularly enough, was known to Wagenseil only as a manuscript, and such it remained until two or three decades ago, when it was printed by a literary society at Stuttgart. In Wagenseil's day it was valued so highly that it was kept wrapped in silk, like the sacred scrolls of the Jews, a circumstance that enabled the pedantic Orientalist to air his learning on the subject for many pages in his wofully discursive but extremely interesting book. But if Wagenseil had not given his testimony, I could now bear witness to the fact that Conrad Nachtigal, Hans Schwartz, Conrad Vogelgesang, Sixtus Beckmesser, Hans Folz, Fritz Kothner, Balthasar Zorn, and Veit Pogner once lived as well as Hans Sachs. I have read some of their poems and copied some of the melodies invented by them and utilized by their successors in the guild. The volumes containing these curiosities of literature have been in the Municipal Library over one hundred years. In the catalogue of the Bibliotheca Norica Williana, printed one hundred and sixteen years ago, they are mentioned as having been purchased from an old master-singer. Five of them are small oblong books of music paper, upon which some old masters or apprentices in the art of master-song have copied melodies which were much used at the meetings in St. Catherine's Church. It was the custom of the members of the guild to compose poems to fit these melodies. In the second scene of his opera Wagner mentions a great many of the singular titles by which these melodies or modes were designated. He got them from Wagenseil. Besides these books, there are two immense manuscript volumes, in which some industrious old lover of the poetical art transcribed songs which he evidently thought admirable. They are each almost as large as Webster's Unabridged Dictionary, and must represent months, if not years, of labor. One is devoted wholly to German paraphrases of Ovid's "Metamorphoses," set to a great variety of melodies. The author is M. Ambrosius Metzger, who was one of the few members of the guild who were scholars. He wrote the poems in 1625. The other volume contains songs by a great number of master-singers, though Hans Sachs is the principal contributor. The plan of the volume indicates that it was a collection of admired poems. It begins with paraphrases from the Pentateuch. Some early pages are missing, the first poem preserved dealing with the sixth chapter of Genesis. Chronological order is maintained up to chapter twenty-eight of the same book. Then follow songs dealing with the Gospels and Epistles. The Book of Job is not forgotten. Finally, there are a number of secular poems, many recounting Æsop's fables and anecdotes drawn from old writers. Songs of this character were composed by the master-singers for diversion at their informal gatherings. At the meetings in the Church of St. Catherine only sacred subjects were allowed. It is for this reason that Wagner's Kothner asks Walther in the opera whether he had chosen sacred matter (*ein heil'gen Stoff*) for his trial song, which provokes the reply from the ardent young knight that he would sing of love, a subject sacred to him. Whether sacred or secular, however, the form and style of the songs are alike. Nothing could more completely illustrate the absurdity of the fundamental theory of the foolish old pedants that poetry might be written by rule of thumb than the publication of a few of the songs in this old book. The nature of the poetical frenzy which fills them can, perhaps, be guessed if I record the fact that the majority of them, I think, begin with a citation of chapter and verse, or some statement equally matter of fact, as thus:

"The twenty-ninth chapter of Genesis records," or "Diogenes, the wise master," or "Strabo writes of the customs," or "Moses, the eleventh, reports," or "The Lesser Book of Truth doth tell," etc.

The last of these lines is the beginning of a master-song which has a twofold interest. In the first place, it is a secular poem by Hans Sachs which, to the best of my knowledge, has never been printed or written about. In the second place, it is set to a melody by the veritable Pogner who, in Wagner's comedy, offers his daughter and his fortune to the winner in the singing contest which makes up Wagner's last act. The poem is so amusing that I would like to give it entire in English, but its irregularity of accent and peculiarities of rhyme do not lend themselves willingly to translation. Of musical accent the master-singers, who followed the rhyming rules of those marvellously ingenious rhymesters the *Minnesinger*, had not the slightest idea. Wagner knew that. Sachs' first critical tap on his lapstone in Beckmesser's serenade is evoked by a blunder in accent which the veritable Sachs would have passed unnoticed, though, being a real poet, his sins in this respect were not as numerous as those of his colleagues and predecessors. I content myself, therefore, with the first *Stollen*, or stanza, and its *Abgesang*, or burden, which the curious student will find to be composed in strict accordance with the rules which, in the opera, Kothner reads from the blackboard. These *Leges Tabulaturæ*, by-the-way, are almost a literal transcription from the original laws preserved in Wagenseil's book. The matter of the song is this: A boor falls ill. Finding that his appetite is wholly gone, he calls in a physician, who informs him (in a drastic fashion) that the trouble is caused by an accumulation of slime in the stomach. He administers a purgative, but without result. The sickness increases, and the boor upbraids the doctor, who retorts that his patient will be a dead man within an hour unless he consent to having his stomach taken out and scoured with chalk. The boor consents, the physician performs the operation, cutting the man open with a pair of shears, brushes out the offending organ with a wisp, and hangs it on the fence to dry. What the farmer does meanwhile is not recorded; but before the physician could replace his stomach a raven carried it off to the woods and ate it. In this dilemma the physician disclosed himself as a worthy progenitor of the modern race of surgeons. He was terribly frightened, but didn't let any one see it. By stealth he procured a sow's stomach, introduced it into the farmer's body, and quickly sewed up the aperture. The farmer got well, and paid eight florins for the job. But heavens, what an appetite was that which he developed! To satisfy him now was utterly impossible, for which reason, concludes the moralist, an insatiable eater is nowadays said to be a hog (literally "to have a sow's stomach"), who devours more than he produces, as many women lament:

"Darum spricht man noch von ein Man,

Den man gar nicht erfuellen kan,

Wie er hab einen Sawmagen;

Verthut mehr denn er gewinnen kan,

Hoert man vil Frawen klagen."

FIRST *STOLLEN*.

[PNG] [Listen]

The Less - er Book of Truth doth tell,
How ill - ness on a boor once fell,
Taste for all food de - stroy - ing;
A - gainst all drugs it did re - bel,
His pleas - ures all al - loy - ing.......

One day there came a doc - tor wise,
Who glanced him o'er with search - ing eyes,
Found out what caused his ail - ing.
His learn - ing proof a - gainst sur - prise,
Made work like that plain sail - ing.......

THE *ABGESANG*.

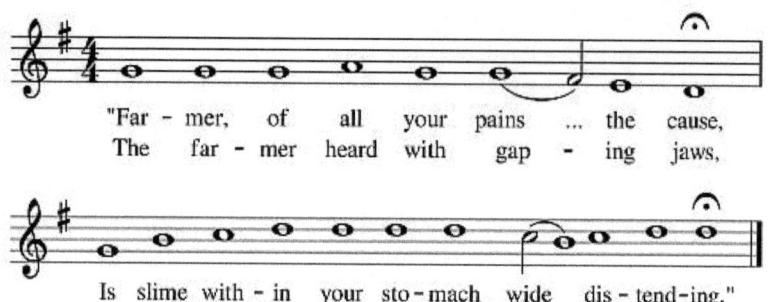

"Far - mer, of all your pains... the cause,
The far - mer heard with gap - - ing jaws,

Is slime with - in your sto - mach wide dis - tend - ing."
For gnaw - ing pains in - side his paunch were rend - ing.

[PNG] [Listen]

"Far - mer, of all your pains... the cause,
Is slime with - in your stom - ach wide dis - tend - ing."
The far - mer heard with gap - - ing jaws,
For gnaw - ing pains in - side his paunch were rend - ing.

The tale is an old one, popular in one form or another in the Middle Ages. A variant of it is to be found in the *Gesta Romanorum*, to which extraordinary collection of moral tales it is possible that Sachs had reference when he spoke of the *Buch der Kleinen Wahrheit*, or Lesser Book of Truth, as I have rendered it. In the *Gesta*, however, the physician substitutes a goat's eye, and subjects his patient to an extraordinary strabismus. Hans Sachs's variation is eminently characteristic of the man and the people for whom he wrote.

CHAPTER IV.
"DER RING DES NIBELUNGEN."

The common error of looking upon the outward covering of things for the things themselves has led to the real plot of Wagner's tetralogical drama "The Niblung's Ring" being overlooked by the majority of persons who have written about it. Especially has the significance of the prologue to the tragedy failed of appreciation. I shall try to tell what I conceive to be the true story of the tragedy, and at least hint at the meaning which that story had when it came into the mind of the sagaman and myth-maker ages ago, which meaning, moreover, Richard Wagner, unlike his modern predecessors among the poets who have treated the subject, apprehended and conserved.

It is a pretty solemn fact that unless this tragedy in four parts be approached with other aims than mere diversion, much will be found in it that appears ridiculous to the judgment, no matter how it affects the senses. To some it may seem a fatal confession to say that sincere and sufficient enjoyment of "The Niblung's Ring" is only to be had by persons willing to let critical judgment wait upon the imagination; yet I am willing to make that confession, and even to augment it by the statement that there are scenes in the tragedy when even this unfettered faculty must needs be as ingenuous as the "raised imagination" of Charles Lamb at his first play, which transformed the glistering substance on the pillars of Old Drury into "glorified sugar-candy." Yet I do not believe that thereby the potential beauty, impressiveness, and significance of the tragedy are brought into question. Is it not easy to conceive of a mental condition which would accept such a childlike receptivity as the only mood in which an art-work designed to appeal to emotions which the humdrum routine of modern life leaves untouched ought to be approached? Wagner's "Ring des Nibelungen" is not an idle fairy-tale, the offspring of a mind working with fanciful material amid the environment of the nineteenth century. It is a tragedy Hellenic in its scope and proportions, dealing with one of the great problems of human existence, reflecting the operations of the quickened mind and conscience of humanity in its impressionable childhood.

"Das Rheingold" is the prologue to a tragedy which has not only the dimensions, but also the aim, of a Greek trilogy. This conception of its dignity greatly widens the significance of its few incidents. Of necessity? Yes. Observe the manner in which Wagner approaches his subject. The hero of the mediæval epic popularly called "The Lay of the Niblung" is Siegfried; and this story of Siegfried is mixed with considerable historical alloy. The character of Gunther, which figures in the story, is Gundikar, founder of the Burgundian monarchy, who was slain by Attila, A.D. 450. Attila himself is one of the personages of the poem, the scene of which plays largely at Worms.

It was Wagner's aim to illustrate a profound truth of universal bearing, and in harmony with his belief that such truths are best taught by presenting pictures of humanity stripped of all conventionality, he went back to the earliest forms of the tale which the mediæval poet wove into the "Lay of the Niblung." By this means he purified it of its historical dross; but also came in contact with the creations of the myth-maker. The period into which he moved his drama was the period reflected by our Northern ancestors when they were striving by an exercise of a vivid imagination and unyielding logic to answer the questions raised by a primitive religious instinct. Whether we want to or not, we must look upon "The Niblung's Ring" as a religious play which, by means of the symbols created by the Northern myth-maker, teaches a lesson universal and eternal in its application.

I.

No legend dealing with the deep passions of human nature, and reflecting the tragic struggle between the human and the divine, which has been playing on the stage of the human heart since the race began, is restricted by the circumstances of time, place, or people. If it is really beautiful and moving it is a bit of universal property, and in one form or another phases of it will be found in the mythology or folk-lore of all civilized peoples. Not only the foundation principles of such a legend, but even its theatre and apparatus may be discovered. Parallels in religious mythologies will readily occur, but perhaps not so readily parallels in those heroic tales which reflect the national characteristics of peoples. Yet they are not the less numerous. The grotto of Venus, in which Tannhäuser steeps himself with sensuality, is but a German form of the Garden of Delight, in which the heroes of classic antiquity met their fair enslavers. It is Ogygia, the Delightful Island, where Ulysses met Calypso. It is that Avalon in which King Arthur was healed of his wounds by his fairy sister Morgain. The staff which bursts into green in the hands of Pope Urban in token of Tannhäuser's forgiveness has prototypes in the lances which, when planted in the ground by Charlemagne's warriors, were transformed over night into a leafy forest; in the staff which put on leaves in the hands of Joseph wherefore the Virgin Mary gave herself to him in marriage; in the rod of Aaron, which, when laid up among others in the tabernacle, "brought forth buds and bloomed blossoms and yielded almonds." The *Tarnhelm* which the cunning Mime fashions at the command of Alberich, what else is it but the Mask of

Arthur, which had the power of rendering its wearer invisible, or the Helmet of Pluto worn by Perseus in his battle with the Gorgon? The Holy Grail, which Wagner has surrounded with such a refulgent halo, is not merely a relic of Christ's suffering and death. Its power of supplying food and sustaining life identifies it with an article common to the mystical apparatus of many peoples. As Achilles was dipped into Styx and rendered invulnerable, so Jason was smeared with Medea's ointment, and Siegfried became covered with a horny armor when he bathed in the dragon's blood; and as the magic wash was kept from Achilles's heel by the hand of Thetis, so the falling of a leaf from a lime-tree on the back of Siegfried caused the one unprotected spot through which a weapon might reach his life. The sword of Wotan, thrust into the tree so firmly and miraculously that none but a hero worthy to wield it and inspired by the desperation of supremest need might draw it from its mighty sheath, what else is it than the "fair sword" which stuck in the marble stone in the church-yard against the high altar, which all the barons assayed in vain to draw forth, but which young Arthur "lightly and fiercely" pulled out of the stone, by which token he was recognized as rightwise king of England? Or, going back further into story-land, who does not see in it that bow of Ulysses which the wicked suitors of Penelope vainly strove to bend, but which yielded to the hero disguised as a beggar with such ease "as a harper in tuning of his harp draws out a string?"

Horus, Apollo, and Baldur in Egypt, Greece, and the savage Northland have represented the highest union of physical and moral excellencies to millions of human beings; and when the Norse myth-maker, exercising his imagination under the influence of that need and longing and hope on which Plato based his argument in proof of the immortality of the soul, drew his picture of Ragnarök, the Twilight of the Gods, the end of the old regime of brute force, of gods and giants, and the return of Baldur and his reign of peace, gentleness, and loveliness, he felt the emotions with which the Christian of to-day looks forward to the second coming of Christ the Redeemer.

So striking are the parallels between the heroic tales of the class to which the story of Siegfried belongs, that it has been possible for Dr. J. G. von Hahn, in his *Sagwissenschaftliche Studien*, to draw up a formula according to which the families belonging to the Aryan race have constructed their most admired tales. This formula, he says, exists more or less perfect in the heroic literature of every known Aryan people. Hellenic mythology produced no less than seven of these stories, of which the most striking are those of Perseus, Theseus, Œdipus, and Herakles; Roman mythological history, one—Romulus and Remus; Teutonic sagas, two—Wittich-Siegfried and Wolfdietrich; Iranian mythic history, two, and Hindu mythology, two, the most striking parallelisms occurring in the story of Krishna. Of this story Mr. Alfred Nutt has found eight variants in old Keltic literature, among them the story of Perceval. According to this formula

I. The hero is born

>(*a*) Out of wedlock.

>(*b*) Posthumously.

>(*c*) Supernaturally

>(*d*) One of twins.

II. The mother is a princess residing in her own country.

III. The father is

(*a*) A god, or

(*b*) A hero

} from afar.

IV. There are tokens and warnings of the hero's future greatness;

V. In consequence of which he is driven from home.

VI. Is suckled by wild beasts.

VII. Is brought up by a childless couple, or shepherd, or widow.

VIII. Is of passionate and violent disposition.

IX. Seeks service in foreign lands.

>(*a*) Attacks and slays monsters.

>(*b*) Acquires supernatural knowledge through eating a fish or other magic animal (the dragon's heart in the case of Sigurd, his blood in the case of Siegfried).

X. Returns to his own country, retreats, and again returns.

XI. Overcomes his enemies, frees his mother, seats himself on a throne.

II.

We should accustom ourselves to look upon the plot of "The Niblung's Ring" as more celestial than terrestrial; the essential things of the tragedy are those which concern Wotan, who is its real hero. The happenings among the personages whose conduct under varying trying circumstances is brought to notice in the three dramas constituting the trilogy are, in reality, but accidents. In this respect "The Niblung's Ring" is in a different case with Homer's *Iliad* which also has a double plot, celestial and terrestrial. The cause of the contest celebrated in the *Iliad* originated on earth; the gods took part in it simply to avenge slights which had been put upon them by one or another of the contestants, or because they were the special protectors of certain of those personages. In Wagner's tragedy the contest waged by the demi-gods, giants, dwarfs, and men, is but the continuation of one invited by the gods. It is the consequence of a sin committed by the chief god and his efforts to repair it. That consequence, in its last and chiefest estate, is the destruction of Wotan and all his fellows; this is what it signifies to all those concerned in it, but to us it means a destruction followed by a new creation. Wotan dies like a tragic hero, and his heroic offspring—the bond connecting gods and men—die one after another, all in consequence of his sin; but the death of the last, being the expiatory self-sacrifice of loving woman, removes the curse from the earth. "Old things are passed away; behold, all things are become new." This is the kernel of the plot of the tragedy, the beginning of which is exhibited in "The Rhinegold," and the outcome prefigured. The progress is from the state of sinlessness, through sin and its awful consequences, to expiation. For each of these steps there are symbols in the pictures, poetry, and music of the prologue.

The gods of our ancestors in the Northland were created in the image of man. Originally the feeling of religion had been satisfied by the conception of a dynasty of gods who, if they were made in the image of man, were at least idealized; they had none of the passions of men, none of their infirmities, none of their trials. When, in later times, the impossibility of such a conception maintaining itself became manifest, humanity among the rugged mountains and in the deep forests of the North dreamed of a time that was past, before the reign of primeval sinlessness and peacefulness had come to an end. That was the Golden Age of the world. Wrong was unknown; the passions which wreck men's lives and beget wrong were unknown; it was the state of Eden before the advent of the tempter. The silence of peace rested upon the waters. Gold was the symbol of radiant innocency; it was but the plaything of the gods. As in Milton's Eden, flowers were of all hue,

> "And without thorn the rose."

> "——Airs, vernal airs,
> Breathing the smell of field and grove, attune
> The trembling leaves, while universal Pan,
> Knit with the Graces and the Hours in dance,
> Led on the eternal Spring."

Put aside the prosaic frame of mind into which the Wolzogen labels are calculated to throw one, and look at the instrumental introduction to the prologue as a symbol of this state of physical and moral loveliness. Could the peacefulness and passionlessness of primeval purity be better typified in music? There are three aspects in which the introduction should be viewed. It is most significant in this study of the tragedy as a type of the Golden Age in Northern mythology. Not until the principle of evil enters the play (in the person of Alberich) is the serenity of the music disturbed.

Next, it is interesting as scenic music. By ingenious use of gauze screens, painted canvas, and light-effects, the stage is made to seem filled with water from floor to flies. Strange plants creep up the side, and gnarled roots project into the water. Below is the rocky bed of the Rhine. Above, a faint light plays on the rippling surface. The music has begun with a single deep tone, but gradually it grows more animated; there is no change in melody, but the introduction of instruments with lighter and lighter tone-color, the introduction and carefully graduated augmentation of a wavy accompaniment, suggest to the ear at once growth in the movement of the water and in the light which shines from above. The music is now doubly delineative. While its spirit reflects the sinless quietude of the Golden Age of the world, its matter depicts, first, the slow movement of the water in its depths, then the gentle undulations of its half-depths, finally the ripples and dartings and flashings and eddyings of its surface.

The third aspect in which we may look at it is as a peculiarly striking exemplification of Wagner's theories of composition carried out to their most logical conclusion. That theory in its extremity would demand that nothing be said when there is nothing to say—a self-evident proposition much oftener honored in the breach than in the observance. Remember that Wagner, in giving an account of the genesis of his typical phrases cites his conduct in "Der Fliegende Holländer," when, having found themes to stand for the mental states described in the ballad, he resolved to repeat its thematic expression every time a mental mood recurred. A necessary corollary of such a logical proceeding would seem to be that until the play had introduced something—a picture, a personage, an idea—there could be no room for music. It is not necessary to go to this extremity; but if we want to we will find that Wagner is true to himself even here. Only the mood of the scene is delineated for us in the music of the introduction, and his willingness to begin as near nothing as possible is shown by the use at the outset of the single deep bass tone. The whole introduction is built on this note and its simplest harmony, the development being accomplished by the gradual changes of orchestration, the employment of higher octaves, and the augmentation of the wavy accompaniment.

III.

It was an inevitable consequence of the structure of the Northern mythological system that the gods should lose their primeval sinlessness. Before the mind of the Northern myth-maker, as before the minds of the Athenians, who erected the altar on Mars-hill "to the Unknown God," there hovered a dim apprehension of a First Cause of all being, older and more puissant than the gods whom he conceived as reigning. As Zeus and his fellows reigned by reason of having overthrown Cronos and the dynasty of the Titans, so Wotan and his fellows reigned by reason of conquest and treaty. In consequence, there was a perpetual struggle between the sky-dwellers, the mountain-dwellers, and the earth-dwellers—the gods, giants, and dwarfs—for dominion. This lust for power it was that caused the downfall of the gods. Dormant within the radiant gold, buried in the Rhine and guarded by the daughters of the Rhine, lay the secret of universal dominion. In the Golden Age no one courted it because there was no need. But when the greed of power and gain asserted itself, the gold was a prize to be sought after and bought at any price. The first change in the stage picture still leaves us the spirit of purity and innocency undisturbed. The Rhine daughters, whose duty it is to guard the magical gold, are careless creatures, as well they may be, for, though warned, they have never seen danger approach their treasure. Floating up and down, they sing and gambol with each other as they swim around the jagged rock, their song being as undulating as the element in which they live. They partake in their nature of that element, and the melodies with which they are associated are imitative of watery movements.

The beginning of the end of the Golden Age was dated by the old poets from the time when three giantesses were admitted among the gods. They were the Nornir, the Fates, whose deep thoughts were given respectively to the past, present, and future. The entrance of a stranger into the domains of the Rhine daughters is also the signal for the introduction of evil into the drama. The representative of this evil principle is Alberich, the Niblung—one of the race of dwarfs; musically his mischievous character, his restless energy, and his strangeness to the element in which he finds himself is told by the orchestra in the abrupt, jerky music to which he enters, and which accompanies his slipping and sliding on the slimy rocks of the river's bottom. Alberich's aims were simply lust. To the nixies he is merely amusing. They engage him in tormenting dalliance till he utters an imprecation against them and shakes his fist. He forgets his anger at his pretty tantalizers, however, when a new spectacle falls upon his sight. The sunlight, piercing the water, has fallen upon the gold, which lies in the cleft of a rock and now begins to glow. The increasing refulgence is seen and heard simultaneously, for as the new light floods the scene, singers and orchestra break out into a ravishing apostrophe to the gold.

Now we reach the point where the ethical contest, at the bottom of the entire tragedy, is first foreshadowed. The nixies, rendered careless by the long uselessness of their watch, prattle away the secret that universal power would be the reward of him who would seize the gold and fashion it into a ring:

"The realm of the world
By him shall be won,
Who from the Rhine gold
Hath wrought the ring,
Imparting measureless might."

But the power to fashion the ring can only be obtained by one willing to renounce the delight and happiness of love:

"Who the delight of Love forswears,
He who derides its ravishing joys,
He alone has the magic might
To shape the gold to a ring."

The issue is joined. Here Love and contentment in the Niblung's lot; there the prospect of power universal and lovelessness. The dwarf does not hesitate long. In the next scene the giants hesitate longer, and Wotan ponders longer than either whether the gold is worth the price demanded for it. But the Age of Innocency is past—all yield in turn to the lust for power, the greed of gain, which the gold promises to satisfy. The first step in the tragedy is taken. Alberich puts love aside forever and curses it. Then, in spite of the shrieks of the nixies, he seizes the gold and dives into the depths.

The light dies out of the scene. The bright song of the nixies runs out into minor plaints, and the orchestra discourses mournfully of the renunciation of love and the rape of the ring, until the scene changes from depths of the Rhine to the heights where Valhalla, newly built, stands in massive strength, gleaming in the morning sun.

We have witnessed the beginning of the struggle for dominion begun cunningly by a dwarf. Not the race of the Niblungs, but the race of giants had caused Wotan concern. Against them he thought to raise an impregnable fortress, and the cunning Loge, the representative of the evil principle in the celestial plot, had contrived to have the work done by two giants, to whom Wotan, at Loge's instigation, promised the goddess Freia as a reward, though Loge had privately assured him that he would never be called on to meet the obligation. The whole tale is borrowed by Wagner from Norse mythology.

Once upon a time, so runs the old story, an artisan came to the gods and offered to build for them a fortress which would forever shield them from the frost giants, if they would give him, in payment, Freya, the goddess of youth, beauty, and love, besides the sun and the moon. The gods agreed, provided he would do the work alone, and in the space of a single winter. When summer was but three days distant the castle was so nearly finished that the gods saw that the compact would be kept by the strange artisan. The imminent loss of Freya frightened the gods, and they threatened Loge with death if he did not prevent the completion of the work within the period fixed. The artisan had the help of a horse named Svadilfari, who drew the most enormous stones to the castle at night. Loge the next night decoyed the horse Svadilfari into the forest, so that the usual quota of work was not done. Then the mysterious workman appeared before the gods in his real form as a giant, and Thor killed him with a blow of his hammer. The Norse Freya is the Teutonic Freia. In Wagner's poem Freia is the reward which the giants Fafner and Fasolt expect for having built Valhalla in a single night. Loge had instigated the compact, and promised to relieve Wotan of the obligation of payment. But the giants carry Freia off and restore her only after Wotan and Loge have given the Niblung's hoard in exchange. To Freia, Wagner has given an attribute which, in Scandinavian mythology, belongs to Iduna. She is the guardian of the golden apples, the eating of which keeps the gods young. Iduna's apples the student of comparative mythology will at once identify with the golden apples which Hera received as a wedding-gift, and which were guarded by the Hesperides and stolen by Hercules. In the Norse story they are carried away by a winged giant named Thiassi, and brought back by Loge, who had tempted Iduna out of her beautiful grove "Always Young," in order that the giant might swoop down upon her and carry the apples away. Wagner gives these apples to Freia for the sake of a dramatic effect. The gods turn wrinkled and gray so soon as the giants carry off the goddess of youth and beauty.

Wotan has his Valhalla, but the giants demand their reward. Loge is summoned to extricate the god from the predicament in which his lust after power has plunged him. The god of fire and the restless representative of the destructive principle appears, and thereafter he is never absent long from the action. He pervades every scene, his red cloak fluttering, eyes, hands, feet, body moving synchronously with that fitful chromatic phrase which crackles and flashes and flickers through the orchestra whenever he takes part in the action. He has searched through the world for a ransom for Freia, and found but one creature who estimated anything higher than the beauty and worth of woman. It is Alberich who, having wrought a ring out of the magic gold, has bent the race of Niblungs to his will, and is now preparing to conquer universal dominion for himself. Thus a new danger threatens the race of gods. In this extremity Wotan listens to the advice of Loge and decides to possess himself of the Niblung hoard, that with it he may purchase the release of Freia, and "make assurance double sure." The two descend to the abode of the dwarfs. In Nibelheim the rocky caverns glow with the reflection of forge fires, and the ear is saluted with the clang of hammers falling upon anvils. Loge cunningly tempts the dwarf to exhibit the magical properties of the *Tarnhelm* (the cap of darkness), and when he assumes the shape of a toad the gods seize and bind him. Under the walls of Valhalla they compel him to ransom himself with gold for the giants and rob him of the ring. Then Alberich burdens it with a curse, introducing into the tragedy the poison which accomplishes the destruction of all its heroes, and remains a bane upon the earth till restitution is made and expiation achieved by the self-immolation of Brünnhilde.

The first fruits of the curse follow hard upon the heels of its utterance. The giants, ravished by the tale of the wealth of the Niblung treasure, exact it all as ransom for Freia. Wotan had aimed to keep the ring as another hostage for the future—with ring and fortress he would feel secure—but the giants demand, the runes upon his spear contain the pledge, and Erda warns. The ring is grudgingly surrendered, and at once its baneful effect is seen. The giants quarrel for its possession, and Fafner kills Fasolt with blows of his staff. Not till then does Wotan realize the deep significance of the warning words of Erda. A solemn duty, an awful task devolves upon him. Murder as well as theft lies at his door; with the ring a fearful curse has entered the world as a consequence of his wrong-doing; henceforth he must devote himself to the work of reparation. Mayhap the wrong may be righted by a restoration of the ring to the original owners of the gold. His own hands are bound, but he conceives a plan, of which the visible symbol is the magic sword. A new race shall arise, the sword shall aid it in obtaining the ring, and of its own will it shall return the circlet to the element from which lust for power wrested it. It is this creative thought which makes him pause with his foot upon the rainbow bridge, across which the celestial household have passed into Valhalla. The sword phrase flashes through the pompous music which is the postlude of the prologue.

IV.

"Höre, höre, höre!
Alles was ist, endet.
Ein düst'rer Tag
Dämmert den Göttern.
Dir rath ich, meide den Ring!"

Thus does Erda warn Wotan. Of all the words of the prologue they are biggest with significance for the tragedy as a whole. They foretell the consequences of Wotan's sin. Erda is the Vala, the goddess of primeval wisdom, "the pantheistic symbol of the universe, the timeless and spaceless mother of gods and men," as Dr. Hueffer calls her. She is the mother of the Nornir. Their phrase is an elemental one, like that of the Rhine. Its ascending intervals suggest growth. The antithesis of this concept is decay, destruction. The melody of the "Twilight of the Gods" (*b*), in the prediction of Erda, appears as an inversion of the elemental melody (*a*).

(*a.*)

[PNG] [Listen]

(*b.*)

[PNG] [Listen]

It is an awful consummation that is predicted by Erda and symbolized in this descending phrase—the destruction of a world as the outcome of that contest which since time began has been the basis of religions and mythologies. No civilized people has escaped being confronted by that problem, but all peoples have not solved it alike. In our own religion the spectacle of its tragical consequences has held the world in awe for nearly nineteen hundred years. Generally in the legends which the human imagination, fired by religious instinct, has created to symbolize the eternal conflict, the hero who goes to destruction is an ideal man. Sometimes he is a god; but only the daring imagination of the Northern myth-maker was equal to the task of making that hero the chiefest of the gods, and connecting his downfall with the end of the race to which he belongs. In this awful flight of the Northern imagination, this sublime achievement of the Northern conscience, lies the essential difference between the religious systems of the classic Greeks and our savage ancestors. The Greeks, profoundly philosophical as they were, would yet have shrunk back appalled from such a solution of the great problem as the Teuton provided in his *Götterdämmerung*. Logic might force them to recognize the necessity of it or something like it, but they would not permit logic to compel them to contemplate it. Once the stern mind of Æschylus seemed on the point of disclosing a divine tragedy approximate in its proportions. Prometheus, chained to the rock on Mount Caucasus, comforts himself in his bitter agony with thoughts of the time when grim necessity shall force Zeus to right his wrongs. But observe that the end of his sufferings is not to follow as an act of retributive justice, but is to be purchased by a compromise. The time will come when Zeus will need his help, for of all the gods Prometheus alone knows how the plot will be laid and how Zeus can escape it:

"I know that Zeus is hard,
And keeps the right supremely to himself;
But then, I know, he'll be
Full pliant in his will
When he is thus crushed down.
Then calming down his mood
Of hard and bitter wrath,
He'll hasten unto me,
As I to him shall haste,
For friendship and for peace."

This is the nearest approach that the Greeks came to a parallel with the most tremendous conception of Northern mythology. Does it strike you as strange? It need not. Remember, the loveliness of their country and climate kept before the Greeks perpetually the benignant aspect of their gods. It is true they found themselves as little able as our ancestors later to maintain these embodiments of a primeval conception of idealized humanity in a state of sinlessness; but when brought face to face with the contradictions which followed, they extricated themselves as best they might by the makeshift of a compromising reconciliation, or flew to the extreme of unbelief. The moral obliquity of the gods was recognized, but was not permitted to throw a shadow over the radiant ones in the Olympian court. You may observe an illustration of this mental trait in the unwillingness of the Greeks to call unpleasant things by their right names. The Euxine, or Hospitable Sea, was once righteously called by them the Axine, or Inhospitable Sea. The dreadful Furies, with their heads covered with writhing snakes, after they had scourged Orestes through the world, were given a temple and worship at Athens as the Eumenides—the kind or good-tempered ones. These Furies belonged to the class of gloomy deities, which was the offspring of conscience and the sense of moral responsibility. They were bound to present themselves to a thinking people, but a people who basked always in Nature's smile were equally bound to subordinate them to the gods of nature that were the embodiment of cheerfulness and light. To contemplate the latter was a delightful occupation; the former were viewed through a veil which concealed their hideousness.

There was nothing in the surroundings of our ancestors to encourage such a species of indirection. The natural powers which confronted them oftenest were inimical. They did not live in the sunlight of Nature's smile, but in the shadow of her frown. The simple right to exist had daily to be conquered. The vague apprehensions of a sinless, an absolute and omnipotent Deity, which flitted furtively across their minds, took deeper and deeper root when the logic of necessity began to taint their dynasty of gods with weakness and crimes. But, like the Greeks, they could give such a conception neither form, habitation, nor name. It remained hovering in the background. As their physical life was a ceaseless struggle with Nature in her sternest aspects, and as the more cruel of those aspects were connected with the phenomena of winter, it was natural that when the conception of overshadowing Fate had to be personified in the process of mythological construction, the Nornir should have been imagined as daughters of the giants of the North—harsh, cruel, vengeful, implacable. The terrible Fimbul winter was to precede Ragnarök. All their training taught them to look the actual in the face. They lived in war, and death possessed terror only to those who could not die in battle. Destruction was a conception with which they were familiar; destruction was the logical outcome of all activities. So soon as they began to contemplate a race of gods who were offenders against that moral law which was the outgrowth of the primitive religious instinct, just so soon such a people had to provide for a catastrophe which would resolve the discord. The Greek tragedian made Prometheus the symbol of humanity and achieved his aim by a reconciliation with offended Deity. The Norse myth-maker chose the chief of the gods as his representative, raised the issue between him and unpersonified moral law, and compelled the god to go down to destruction with all his race to satisfy a vast and righteous necessity. "If," says Felix

Dahn, "a religion has become thoroughly corrupt, then, unless the nation professing it is to be destroyed along with its civilization, a new religion, satisfying to the needs of the period, must either be introduced from without—as Christianity was introduced in the Roman world in the first centuries of the Empire—or the existing religion must be purified and reconstructed; as was the case with Christianity in the sixteenth century through the Protestant Reformation, and also, indeed, through the very material Catholic improvements achieved by the Tridentine Council.

"But beside these two there is a third means of resolving the difficulty; this third was seized upon by the Germanic consciousness. *It is the tragical remedy.*

"The Germanic gods, too, placed themselves in irreconcilable and unendurable opposition to morality; and the Germanic conscience condemned them every one to destruction—to death! *That is the meaning of the Götterdämmerung;* it is a peerlessly great moral deed of the Germanic race, and it stamps Germanic mythology with its tragic character.

"Destruction because of an irreparable rupture with established and peaceful order in Religion, Morality, or Law, is essentially tragical.

"The *Götterdämmerung* a sacrifice? A stupendous deed of morality? Aye, indeed, that it is!"[D]

V.

We are henceforth to observe Wotan in his conduct when brought face to face with the consequences of his violations of moral law. That conduct it is which reflects the real tragedy in "The Niblung's Ring." Bound by the contract whose runes were cut in the haft of his spear, the god could not again possess himself of the ring, which was now become doubly a menace. If it were again to fall into the hands of Alberich, whom he had so cruelly wronged, the desire for vengeance would spur that mischievous Niblung to seize the dominion which had been forfeited. To prevent such a catastrophe, Wotan would beget a new race of beings and endow them with a magic sword. This was to be the extent of his activity in the development of his plot. As a Volsung he wandered through the forests with Siegmund, his son born of woman. At an early age this son had lost his mother and been separated from his twin-sister. Then his father left him mysteriously to be seasoned to his task by hardships. At the climax of his distress, the culmination of his need, he was to arm himself with the divine sword which the god had thrust up to the hilt in a tree, around which was built the hut of that very enemy of the Volsung race, who had carried off the sister and married her against her will. The achievement of the sword was to be the sign of Siegmund's fitness for the enterprise. Of his own free-will the divinely-begotten hero was to acquire the ring, and rid the world of the curse by restoring it to its rightful owners. How vain a plot! The first step in its development shatters the whole elaborate fabric! Both of the children forfeit their lives to outraged law; the god is compelled to destroy the very agencies on which he had built his hopes. The curse under whose fatal influence he had fallen because of wrong-doing was not to be averted by so shallow a subterfuge; but even if such an outcome had been possible, the plan would have split on the rock of newly offended morality.

In this outline of the contents of "Die Walküre" I have but hinted at its incidents, yet we have before us a whole vast act of the Wotan tragedy, and one, too, that is pregnant with consequences to the tragical scheme of the myth-maker. I do not ask that the occasional interpretations of Wagner's music which I attempt be accepted as literal expositions of the composer's purposes; but we can benefit in our understanding of the scope and progress of his tragedy by discovering symbols for its great philosophical moments in the musical investiture. In this view of the case observe how appropriate is the instrumental introduction to the first act. We have gone beyond the hand-books in seeing a reflection of the purity and quietude of the Golden Age in the introduction to the prologue. Its antithesis is presented in the introduction to the first drama of the trilogy. Again Wagner makes nature reflect the mental and moral states of his personages. Again he presents a musical mood-picture. And again the musician is invited to discover that, in spite of the contrast between the objects of his musical delineation, the technical means resorted to are the same. There the peacefully undulating *major* harmonies over a sustained bass note—a pedal-point, if you will—pictured the age of sinlessness; the harmlessness of the untainted, uncoveted virgin gold; the gentle flux and reflux of the element in which it was buried; the careless innocency of its unsuspicious and playful guardians. Here wildly flying *minor* harmonies under a sustained note—again a pedal-point—picture the storm which buffets the exhausted, unprotected Siegmund, and impels him to seek refuge in Hunding's hut.

If this parallel is merely fanciful, it at least invites such an exercise of the fancy in the listeners as will better help them to appreciate the interdependence of the arts which Wagner consorts in his dramas than any amount of structural dissection and analysis. If you wish you may note that in addition to the music which aims merely at imitative delineation of a thunder-storm (the rushing figure in the basses, the incessant *staccato* patter of the sustained note, the attempts to suggest flashes of lightning in short and rapid figures in the high register of the instruments, the crashing and rumbling of thunder, and the howling of the wind in the chromatic passages), the music also presents a pompous phrase with which, in the scene of the prologue where Thor created the rainbow bridge, the

Thunderer summoned the elements to his aid, and at the close a heavy-footed phrase which may be identified with the weary Siegmund.

If these two preludes be accepted as broadly and comprehensively delineative of moods in the theatre and personages of the play, another significant parallel will now present itself. It was to a phrase which has the rhythm afterwards associated with the Niblungs in their capacity as smiths (see Chapter I.)—the hammering rhythm—that Alberich disclosed his wicked nature and resolve when he shook his fist at the nixies. Observe how the element of danger to the Volsung pair is introduced in the first scene of the tragedy. It enters with the sinister Hunding, who, as the unconscious instrument of Fate and Fricka's vengeance, brings death to Siegmund. In the music which precedes Hunding's entrance there are only strains of pathetic tenderness which invite sympathy for the unhappy children of Wotan, and which we are asked by the analyst and commentator to associate with the compassion which they feel for each other, and the growth of that feeling into the more ardent emotion of love. The phrase which ushers in Hunding is in sharp contrast; if is gloomy in harmony and orchestration, and publishes the evil in his heart, not only by its dark colors, but also by employing the threatening rhythm which Alberich used against the Rhine daughters. The incidents which serve to complete the first great step in the drama so far as Wotan, the hero, is concerned, can now be hastily reviewed. Hunding discovers his guest to be the enemy of his race; the laws of hospitality protect him for the night, but he must fight on the morrow. Siegmund's need has reached its climax. But Sieglinde, after putting Hunding to sleep with a draught, returns to him and discloses the mystery of the sword. Mutually they confess their love, and discover their relationship in the moment when the magic sword is won. A new thought prevents that terrible discovery from checking the progress of their passion. *The race of the Volsungs must be perpetuated.* If you want to learn how powerful an element this thought is in the old legend from which Wagner borrowed the episode, you must study it in the Volsunga Saga, where it is consorted with elements which largely atone for the features so offensive and so much criticised in Wagner's drama. There Signy (Wagner's Sieglinde) desiring to avenge herself on her husband Siggeir (Hunding), who had murdered all the race but her and Sigmund, and kept her in loveless wedlock, tried in vain to rear a son of sufficient hardihood to perform the deed of vengeance. At last, fearful that the Volsungs might become extinct, she changed semblance with a witch-wife, and in this guise visited Sigmund at his hiding-place in the woods. When their son grew to manhood he and his father avenged Signy's wrongs. But when they offered her great honors Signy told Sigmund: "I went into the woods to thee in witch-wife's shape, and Sinfjötli (Siegfried) is the son of thee and me both; and therefore has he this great hardihood and fierceness, because he is the son of Välse's son and Välse's daughter. For naught else have I so wrought that King Siggeir might get his bane at last; and merrily now will I die with the King though I was naught merry to wed him;"[E] and she entered the burning palace and died with the King and his men. The motive here is the same as in the objectionable episode in Wagner, but it is presented more forcibly and, at the same time, less offensively—or, at least, with less show of moral depravity. But the sin is speedily expiated. Fricka, the patron goddess of marriage, demands that Siegmund shall become her victim; and Fricka's right cannot be gainsaid by the representative of Law. Wotan pronounces the oath that Fricka demands. The Volsung is doomed; the plan of the god frustrated. The first act of the tragedy is complete; the second stage of the development of Wotan's tragical character is entered upon. These are the essential features of that stage:

In despair the god surrenders his plan, invokes the consequences of his guilty deed, and pronounces a blessing on the inimical agency which has been established for his punishment. He turns his longing gaze towards that outcome of the terrible conflict in which he became involved because of his greed of power, which his own wisdom, clarified by the mystic words of Erda, recognizes as inevitable.

Unhappily for the popular understanding of the tragedy, the scene in which this stupendously significant phase in the celestial action of the drama is disclosed is one that is generally sacrificed to theatrical exigencies. It is presented in the long address in which Wotan countermands the order previously given for the death of Hunding, and commands that the death-mark be placed on Siegmund. From this recital we learn that the Valkyrior had been born to Wotan by Erda as part of his scheme to perpetuate his dominion. They were to fill Valhalla with heroes against the great battle which he knew would come. We also learn that as Wotan had begotten a new race, in the hope of preventing the baneful ring from falling again into the hands of Alberich, so Alberich, in turn, had begotten a son to labor for its return. But as Alberich had foresworn love, he wooed a woman with gold. Again, here in the counter-plot, the greed of gold usurps the place sanctified to love. Thus there are pitted against each other the Volsungs, beloved progeny of the god, and Hagen (whom we shall meet actively engaged in the contest later), the loveless offspring of the Niblung. And the demi-god it is who is doomed. Wotan is called upon to perform his act of renunciation. As things go in the theatre, his recital is thought overlong and undramatic, and the thoughtless laugh at the spectacle of a sad god. Can we forget that it is at this supreme moment that the god embodies that which is at once the loftiest and the most profoundly melancholy conception of the Germanic conscience? He recognizes the necessity and the justice of the destruction of his race. Listen to his words:

"Begone, then, and perish,
Thou gorgeous pomp,
Thou glittering disgrace
Of godhood's grandeur!
Asunder shall burst
The walls I built!
My work I abandon,
For one thing alone I wish—
The end—
The end—"

(*He pauses in thought.*)

"And to the end
Alb'rich attends!
Now I perceive
The secret sense
Of the Vala's 'wildering words:
 'When Love's ferocious foe
In rage begetteth a son,
The night of the gods
Draws near anon.'"[F]

And now observe how the logic of Wagner's constructive scheme marshals the symbols of the chief things which are in Wotan's thoughts while he contemplates past, present, and future—the wicked cause and the terrible effect. The curse, with death in its train, confronts him:

[PNG] [Listen]

the Nomir and their all-wise mother revisit his fancy:

[PNG] [Listen]

the ceaseless, tireless energy of the Niblung, which will not cease till the work of destruction be complete, pursues him with its rhythmical scourge as the Furies pursued Orestes:

[PNG] [Listen]

and the image of Valhalla rises in his far-seeing mind, not as a castle in its present grandeur (see Chapter I.), but in ruins; the rhythm of the musical symbol is shattered; its solid, restful, simple major harmony is destroyed:

[PNG] [Listen]

All this because of the accursed gold (closing cadence *a*).

The daughter to whom the god confides the whole depth of his misery is of all his daughters the dearest. She has no higher ambition than to be the embodiment of Wotan's will. Unconsciously to both, the god, in his divine resignation, is merely prefiguring the sacrifice to which, in the providence of a higher power than the Lord of Valhalla, that daughter has been chosen. But the god has not yet learned the full bitterness of his cup. He loves the Volsung, and is obliged to destroy at a blow the object of his love and the agent of his plan. In doing this the irresistible might of law bears down his will. That will is known to Brünnhilde. In defiance of Wotan's commands she attempts to shield the Volsung; and to bring the combat between Hunding and Siegmund to the conclusion inexorably demanded by that law of purity which the hero unwittingly violated, the god is himself compelled to interfere, and to cause the sword, designed as the symbol of the Volsung power, to be shattered on the spear with which Wotan exercises dominion.

Love, for a second time, feels the weight of Alberich's curse. Now the beloved daughter falls under the condemnation of the law. But the god is becoming unconsciously an agent in a plan of redemption, which belongs to a loftier ethical scheme than was possible before. Wotan is about to disappear as an active agent from the scene. His plot is wrecked. The representative of his will, the object of his tenderest paternal affection, unknown to him, but inspired wholly by a love void of all selfishness, is about to take up the task surrendered by the god, and carry it out to a conclusion different from and yet like that imagined by the god. Before the punishment is visited upon her, the intensity of that love, turned through sympathy towards Sieglinde, has for a moment endowed her with prophetic powers. She hails the hero yet unborn, and persuades Sieglinde to save her own life for his sake. Then she accepts her punishment. She is bereft of her divinity, put into a magic sleep, and left by the way-side to be the prey of the first passer-by. But the love of the father, awakened to tenfold power by the bitterness of his own fate and the knowledge that his child's disobedience was but the execution of his own will, shields her from dishonor by surrounding her with a wall of fire, which none but a freer hero than the god himself, and one for whom the divine spear has no terrors, shall pass. The god's egotism is completely broken, the reconciliation between his offended majesty and the offender established. The punishment of Brünnhilde is but the chastisement of love. Can there be any doubt of this after the musical proclamation contained in the finale of "Die Walküre?"

VI.

I am presuming, to a great extent, upon the reader's familiarity with the incidents of the dramas constituting the tragedy. It is the action which takes place where we have not been in the habit of looking for it that I am seeking to discover. "Siegfried," the second drama of the trilogy, is almost wholly devoted to preparation for the fateful outcome. To this fact is due much of its cheerfulness of tone. It is a period of comparative rest. The celestial plot has entered upon a new phase, and in this drama the new combination of characters is formed for the development of that new phase. The ethical drama which the play symbolizes might be described as follows:

The hero has been born and bred under circumstances which have developed his freedom in every direction. The representative of the evil principle seeks to direct his heroic powers towards an advancement of the sinister side of the counter-plot; but in vain. By his own efforts he endows himself with the magic sword, and in the full consciousness of his free manhood he achieves for himself the adventures and the happiness which were denied to the god. He gains the ring and tastes the delight of love.

At first Siegfried appears simply as a wild forest lad, who has grown up with no sympathetic acquaintance beyond the beasts and birds with which he is wont to associate in their haunts. In this character the composer pictures him musically by means of the merry hunting-call which he is supposed to blow on his horn (see Chapter I.). Most of the music which is associated with him in the first act of the drama, in which this horn-call enters so largely, is markedly characteristic of the impetuous nature of the forest lad, with his contempt for dissimulation and his rough, straightforward energy. But a different side of his nature is disclosed when, having learned the story of his birth and acquired possession of his father's sword, remade by himself, he becomes a part of the sylvan picture of the second act, which lends so much charm to the "Siegfried" drama. Here, again, is scenic music of the kind which each of the dramas possesses, and which has so often set us to wondering at Wagner's marvellous faculty for juggling with the senses—making our ears to see and our eyes to hear. Siegfried has been brought before the cave—where Fafner, in the form of a dragon, is guarding the ring and the hoard—by Mime, who has planned that the lad shall kill the dragon and then himself fall a victim to treachery. Siegfried throws himself on a hillock at the foot of a tree and listens to nature's music in the forest. And such music! Music redolent of that sweet mystery which peopled the old poets' minds with the whole amiable tribe of fays and dryads and wood-nymphs. The spirit which lurks under gnarled roots and in tangled boughs, in hollow trees and haunted forest caves, breathes through it. The youth is brooding over the mystery of his childhood, and he utters his thoughts in tender phrases, while the mellow wood-wind instruments in the orchestra identify his thoughts with the dead parents whom he never knew. He wonders what his mother looked like, and pathetically asks whether all human mothers die when their children are born. Suddenly the sunlight begins to flicker along the leafy canopy; a thousand indistinct voices join in that indefinable hum, of which, when heard in reality and not in the musician's creation, one is at a loss to tell how much is actual and how much the product of imagination, both sense and fancy having been miraculously quickened by the spirit which moves through the trees.

At last all is vocal, and Siegfried's ear is caught by the song of the bird to which we too have been listening. In his longing for companionship he wishes that he might understand and converse with his feathered playmate. Might he not if he were able to whistle like the bird? Now note the naïve touch of musical humor with which Wagner, the tragedian, enlivens the scene. Siegfried cuts a reed growing beside a rivulet and fashions a rude pipe out of it. He listens, and when the bird quits singing he attempts to imitate its "wood-note wild." But his pipe is too low in pitch and out of tune. He cuts it shorter and raises its pitch half a tone. Again he cuts it, with the same result; then squeezes it impatiently, and renders it still more "out of tune and harsh." He throws it away, confesses his humiliation by the bird, then reaches for his horn. With its merry call he wakes the echoes, disturbs the sleep of the dragon, and precipitates the combat which ends in his equipment with *Tarnhelm* and ring, and his receipt of the injunction from the bird (which now he understands through the magic of the dragon's blood touching his lips) to slay Mime and waken Brünnhilde on the burning mountain.

We now catch our last glimpse of Wotan as a personage in the play. He has not been active in the plot since he was obliged to destroy his own handiwork. Twice he appeared in the character of a seemingly unconcerned spectator wandering over the face of the earth, and once he even offered to help Alberich recover the ring from Fafner. He aroused the dragon and suggested that Alberich warn him of threatened danger, and ask the ring as a reward. His present concern is to learn whether the danger threatening the gods is yet to be averted. By chanting of powerful runes he summons Erda, of ancient wisdom. But she refuses to speak. Now he tells her that he no longer grieves over the approaching doom of the gods; his will, newly enlightened, has decreed that the catastrophe shall overwhelm the gods, but also that the world, which in his despair he had surrendered to the hate of the Niblung, shall become instead the heritage of the Volsung who has won the ring. A single act remains to be done: the free-agency of Siegfried must be tested. The youth follows his feathered guide up the mountain to find the promised bride. Wotan bars his way with his spear. Siegfried hews the shaft through the middle. On the runes cut into that shaft rested Wotan's dominion. They were the bond by which he governed. Its destruction symbolizes the approaching end of the old order of things. The musical phrase, typical of that compact, accompanies him, in broken rhythm, as he gathers up the pieces of the spear and departs. Prophecy and fulfilment are indicated by the recurrence of the phrase of Erda and her daughters, the Nornir, and its inversion, which symbolizes the twilight of the gods.

VII.

All the adventures of Siegfried in this part of the drama, from the forging of the sword to the awaking of Brünnhilde, Wagner derived in almost the exact shape in which he presents them from the Scandinavian legends which tell of Sigurd. In the death-like sleep of Brünnhilde, the stream of fire around her couch, the passage of that stream by Siegfried, as later in the immolation of the heroine, there are so many foreshadowings of the mystery of the Atonement that I scarcely dare attempt a study of it. Let me but call attention to the fact that the fiery wall in the old legends always denotes the funeral pyre; that it was once customary to light the pyre with a thorn, and that when the Eddas tell us that Odin put his child Brynhild to sleep by pricking her in the temple with a sleep-thorn, the meaning is that she died. I have said a foreshadowing of the Atonement because these things are old Aryan possessions—much older than Christianity. The infernal river of the Greeks, which Alkestis had to cross when she went to the under-world on her mission of salvation, had a Greek name (*Pyriphlegethon*), which meant "fire-blazing." It was not, however, to lose myself in such speculations that I called up the old story, but simply to show with what fine insight into dramatic possibilities Wagner studied his sources. In the old Icelandic tale, some gossiping eagles, whose language Sigurd had come to understand by drinking of the blood of Regin and Fafnir, told him of a maiden who slumbered in a hall on high Hindarfiall surrounded with fire. Thither Sigurd went, penetrated the barrier of fire, found Brynhild, whom he thought to be a knight until he had ripped up her coat of mail with his sword, and awakened her. Learning the name of her deliverer, Brynhild cried out:

"Hail to thee, Day, come back!

Hail, sons of the Daylight!

Hail to thee, daughter of night!

Look with kindly eyes down

On us sitting here lonely,

And give us the gain that we long for."[G]

VIII.

We reach the last drama of the trilogy.

In the joy of his new-found love Siegfried forgets his mission. Brünnhilde teaches him wisdom (recall how the ancient Teutons reverenced the utterance of their women), and he gives her the baneful circlet as the badge of his love. He goes out in search of adventure, and, separated from the protecting influence of woman's love, he falls a victim to the wiles of Hagen, the Niblung's son. Alberich had warned Hagen that so great was Siegfried's love for Brünnhilde that were she to ask it he would restore the ring to the Rhine nixies. This must be prevented, and Hagen has a plan ready. With a magic drink he robs Siegfried of all memory of Brünnhilde, and the hero, to gain a new love, puts on his *Tarnhelm* and rudely drags Brünnhilde from her flame-encircled retreat.

To Wagner's skill in expressing the miraculous in music is due the effectiveness of two scenes highly essential to the ethical scheme of the tragedy and very difficult to present in a dramatic form. The music accompanying the drink alone makes it possible to realize that the fateful change has taken place in Siegfried. He looks into the horn and pledges Brünnhilde:

"Were I to forget
All thou gav'st,
One lesson I'll never

Unlearn in my life.
This morning-drink,
In measureless love,
Brünnhild, I pledge to thee!"[H]

Niemann puts the horn from his lips, and we know that a change has taken place in the man. It is the mystical property of that weird music that brings us this consciousness. We could not believe it if acts or words alone were relied on to make the publication.

Again has love been wronged. The guilt of a tragic hero may be unconsciously committed; still he must yield to fate. Chance puts the opportunity in the way of Siegfried to prevent the ring from falling into the hands of the powers inimical to the gods; but he proudly puts it aside because the demand of the Rhine daughters was coupled with a threat. Brünnhilde had also spurned the opportunity, but in her case the motive was her great love for Siegfried, which made her prize the ring, as its visible sign, above the welfare of the gods. That love, misguided, causes the death of the hero. Brünnhilde, learning of Siegfried's unconscious treachery, gives her aid to the Niblung's son. Only his death clears away the mystery. Then she expiates her crime and his with her life, and from her ashes the Rhine daughters recover the ring.

"The ultimate question concerning the correctness or effectiveness of Wagner's system must be answered along with the question, Does the music touch the emotions, quicken the fancy, fire the imagination? If it does this we may, to a great extent, if we wish, get along without the intellectual process of reflection and comparison conditioned upon a recognition of his themes and their uses. But if we do this, we will also lose the pleasure which it is the province of memory sometimes to give;"[I] for a beautiful constructive use of the themes is for reminiscence. The culminating scene of the tragedy furnishes us an illustration of the twofold delight which Wagner's music can give: the simply sensuous and the sensuous intensified by intellectual activity. I refer to the death of Siegfried. As Siegfried, seated among Gunther's men, who are resting from the chase, tells the story of his life, we hear a recapitulation of the musical score of the second and third acts of "Siegfried" the drama. He starts up in an outburst of enthusiasm as he reaches the account of Brünnhilde's awaking, which is interrupted by the flight of Wotan's ravens, who go to inform the god that the end is nearing. He turns to look after the departing birds, when Hagen plunges a spear into his back. The music to which the hero, regaining his memory, breathes out his life, is that ecstasy in tones to which Siegfried's kiss had inspired the orchestra in the last scene of the preceding drama. Why is this? Because, as Siegfried's last thoughts before taking the dreadful draught which robbed him of his memory were of Brünnhilde, so his first thoughts were of her when his memory was restored. Before his dying eyes there is only the picture of her awaking, till the last ray of light bears to him Brünnhilde's greeting:

"Brünnhild!

Hallowed bride!

Awaken! Open thine eyes!

Who again has doomed thee

To dismal slumber?

Who binds thee in bonds of sleep?

The awakener came,

His kiss awoke thee;

Once more he broke

The bonds of his bride;

Then shared he Brünnhild's delight!

Ah! those eyes

Are open forever!

Ah! how sweet

Is her swelling breath!

Delicious destruction—

Ecstatic awe—

Brünnhild gives greeting—to me!"

This reminiscent love-music gives way to the Death March, which, from a purely structural point of view, is an epitome of much that is salient in the musical investiture of the entire tetralogy, yet in spirit is a veritable apotheosis, a marvellously eloquent proclamation of antique grief and heroic sorrow. This music loses nothing in being listened to as absolute music. Never mind that in obedience to his system of development Wagner has passed the life of Siegfried in review in the score. The orchestra has a nobler mission here. It is to make a proclamation which neither singers nor pantomimists nor stage mechanism and pictures can make.

The hero is dead!

What does it mean to him?

Union with Brünnhilde—restoration to that love of which he had been foully robbed.

What to his fellows in the play?

The end of a Teutonic hero of the olden kind. He is dead; they are awed at the catastrophe and they grieve; but their grief is mixed with thoughts of the prowess of the dead man and the exalted state into which he has entered. A Valkyria has kissed his wounds, and Wotan has made place for him at his board in Valhalla. There, surrounded by the elect of Wotan's wishmaidens, he is drinking mead and singing songs of mighty sonority—Viking songs like Ragnar Lodbrok's: "We smote with swords."

Is there room here for modern mourning; for shrouding crape and darkened rooms and sighs and tears and hopeless grief? No. The proper expression is a hymn, a pæan, a musical apotheosis; and this is what Wagner gives us until the funeral train enters Gutrune's house and the expression of sorrow goes over to the deceived wife.

But what does this march mean to us who have been trying to study the real meaning of the tragedy? The catastrophe which is to usher in the new era of love. Search for a musical symbol for the redeeming principle. It cannot appear in its fulness till the old order, changing, gives place to the new; but still we may find it in the prevision of a woman to whom the shadow of death gave mystical lore. A new song was put into the mouth of Sieglinde when Brünnhilde acclaimed her child, yet unborn, as destined to be the loftiest hero of earth. She poured out her gratitude in a prophetic strain in which we may, if we wish, hear the Valkyria celebrated as the loving, redeeming woman of the last portion of the tragedy. Out of that melody, and out of a phrase in the love duet in which Brünnhilde blesses the mother who gave birth to the glorious hero, grew the phrase in which, in "Die Götterdämmerung," Brünnhilde, Valkyria no longer, is symbolized in her new character as loving woman. But when the flames from Siegfried's funeral pile reach Valhalla, when by a stupendous achievement the poet-composer recapitulates the incidents of the tragedy in his orchestral postlude, while pompous brass and strident basses depict the destruction of Valhalla, the end of the old world of greed of gold and lust of power, this melody, the symbol of redeeming love, soars high into ethereal regions on the wings of the violins, and its last transfigured harmonies proclaim the advent of a new heaven and a new earth under the dominion of love. 'Tis the "Woman's Soul" leading us "upward and on:"

[PNG] [Listen]

FOOTNOTES:

[D] *Walhall. Germanische Götter und Heldensagen.* Felix Dahn and Therese Dahn. Kreutznach, 1888.

[E] *Vide* Magnusson and Morris.

[F] Professor Dippold's translation.

[G] Dippold. Wagner's poem, "The Ring of the Nibelung," p. 61.

[H] Professor Dippold's translation.

[I] See page 35.

CHAPTER V.
"PARSIFAL."

The last of Wagner's dramas is not only mystical in its subject, but also in the manner in which it confronts the critical student. In Bayreuth it exerts a most puissant influence upon the spectator and listener; but when one has escaped the sweet thraldom of the representation, and reflection takes the place of experience, there arise a multitude of doubts touching the essential merit of the drama. These doubts do not go to the effectiveness of "Parsifal" as an artistic entertainment. If they did they would arise in the course of the representation and hinder enjoyment. Against what, then, do they direct themselves?

An answer to this question must precede our study of the drama.

I.

"Parsifal" is not a drama in the ordinary acceptation of the term; yet it is a drama in the antique sense. It is a religious play; but, again, not a religious play in the general sense in which Wagner's mythological tetralogy may be said to be a religious play; it is specifically a Christian play. It is contemplation of it in this light which gives the student pause. There are indications in the records of Wagner's intellectual activity that he wrote it to take the place of two dramas which had occupied his mind many years before "Parsifal" was written. The first of these dramas, which he sketched in 1848, was a tragedy entitled "Jesus of Nazareth;" the second, which he planned in 1856, was entitled "The Victors," and was based on a Hindu legend. Its hero was to be Chaka-Munyi—the Buddha. In a manner, it may be said, these two dramas were blended in "Parsifal," but, strangely enough, that blending was accomplished so as to bring into prominence a conception of religion more in harmony with the feeling of Buddhistic, or mediæval asceticism than with the sentiments of modern Christianity. Wagner's Jesus of Nazareth was a purely human philosopher who preached the saving grace of love, and sought to redeem his time from the domination of conventional law—the offspring of selfishness. His philosophy was socialism imbued with love. Wagner's Buddha, on the other hand, was the familiar apostle of abnegation and asceticism. The heroism of the lovers Ananda and Prakriti was to have been displayed in their voluntary renunciation of the union, towards which love impelled them. They were to accept the teachings of the Buddha, take the vow of chastity, and live thereafter in the holy community.

When Wagner came to write his Christian drama he put aside his human Christ, accepted the doctrine of the Atonement with all its mystical elements, but endowed his hero with scarcely another merit than that which had become the ideal of monkish theologians under the influence of fearful moral depravity and fanatical superstition, as far removed from the teachings and example of his original hero as the heavens are from the earth. After having eloquently proclaimed the ethical idea which is at the basis of all the really beautiful mythologies and religions of the world, and embodied it in "The Flying Dutchman," "Tannhäuser," and "The Niblung's Ring"—the idea that salvation comes to humanity through the redeeming love of woman—he produced a drama in which the central idea, so far as the dramatic spectacle is concerned, is a glorification of a conception of sanctity which grew out of a monstrous perversion of womanhood, and a wicked degradation of womankind.

This, I say, is the case "so far as the dramatic spectacle is concerned." Of course there is much more in "Parsifal" than a celebration of the principal feature in mediæval asceticism, but I am speaking now of the things which fill the vision during representation, which inspire a feeling of awe at the time, but afterwards irritate and confound the reflective faculty. So far as the spectacle is concerned, the heroism of Parsifal is not that of the Divine Being, of whom Wagner does not hesitate to make him a symbol, but that of a desert recluse. This contradiction of the modern sense of propriety is accentuated by the means resorted to by Wagner for the sake of identifying the hero with his lofty prototype. In the third act, scenes are borrowed from the life of Christ, and Parsifal is made to play in them as the central figure; Kundry anoints the feet of the knight and dries them with her hair; Parsifal baptizes Kundry and absolves her from sin. These acts, and the resistance of Kundry's seductions in the Magic Garden, make up, for the greater part, the sum of the acts of a hero in whom the spectator wishes to see, on the one hand, some of the attributes of the heroes of the profoundly poetical romances from which the subject-matter of the drama was drawn, or, on the other, some evidences of that nobility and that gentleness of conduct, and that fine sanity of thought which marked the life of Him of whom it has been said that he was

"The best of men
That e'er wore earth about him—
A soft, meek, patient, humble, tranquil spirit,
The first true gentleman that ever breathed."

These things, taken in connection with the adoration of the Holy Grail, which makes up so much of the action of the drama, and the worship of the Sacred Lance, seem to us of the nineteenth century like little else than relics of the monkish superstitions of the early Middle Ages. Under them, it is true, there is much deep philosophy, and the symbolism of the drama is surcharged with meaning; but a recognition of the paradox is necessary, the better to appreciate the fact that the essence of "Parsifal" lies less in what is seen on the stage than in what the things seen stand for. To appreciate the work at its full worth it must be accepted for the lesson which it inculcates, and that lesson must be accepted in the spirit of the time which produced the materials of the drama. The ethical idea of the drama is that it is the enlightenment which comes through conscious pity that brings salvation. The allusion is to the redemption of man by the sufferings and compassionate death of Christ; and that stupendous tragedy is the prefiguration of the mimic tragedy which Wagner has constructed. The spectacle to which he invites us, and with which he hopes to impress us and move us to an acceptance of the lesson underlying his drama, is the adoration of the Holy Grail, cast in the form of a mimicry of the Last Supper, bedizened with some of the glittering pageantry of mediæval knighthood and romance. The trial to which the hero is subjected is that with which the folk-lore of all times and peoples, as well as their monkish legends, have made us familiar: the hero proves his fitness for his divine calling, and accomplishes it by withstanding the temptations which Ulysses withstood on the Delightful Island where he met Calypso, to which Tannhäuser succumbed in the grotto of Venus.

Though "Parsifal" endures a separation of its poetic, scenic, and musical elements less graciously than any other drama of its creator, it is the music which must be relied on to bring about a reconciliation between modern thought and feeling, and the monkish theology and relic worship which I have discussed. The music reflects the spirit of that Divine Passion which is the kernel of theological Christianity. There is extremely little music in the score, which is descriptive of external things—less than in any other of Wagner's works except "Die Meistersinger." It is like that of "Tristan und Isolde," which deals much more with mental and psychic states than with the outward things of nature. It is music for the imagination rather than the fancy. In listening to it one can be helped by bearing in mind the distinction so beautifully made by Ruskin:

"The fancy sees the outside, and is able to give a portrait of the outside, clear, brilliant, and full of detail.

"The imagination sees the heart and inner nature, and makes them felt, but is often obscure, mysterious, and interrupted in its giving out of outer detail.

"Fancy, as she stays at the externals, can never feel. She is one of the hardest-hearted of the intellectual faculties, or, rather, one of the most purely and simply intellectual. She cannot be made serious, no edge-tool but she will play with; whereas the imagination is in all things the reverse. She cannot be but serious; she sees too far, too darkly, too solemnly, too earnestly ever to smile. There is something in the heart of everything, if we can reach it, that we shall not be inclined to laugh at.

"Now observe, while as it penetrates into the nature of things, the imagination is pre-eminently a beholder of things as they are, it is, in its creative function, an eminent beholder of things when and where they are not; a seer, that is, in the prophetic sense, calling the things that are not as though they were; and forever delighting to dwell on that which is not tangibly present.... Fancy plays like a squirrel in its circular prison and is happy; but imagination is a pilgrim on the earth, and her home is in heaven."

The fundamental elements of the music of "Parsifal" are suffering and aspiration. When they are apprehended the ethical purpose of the drama becomes plain. But not till then.

II.

The investigations of scholars determined long ago that the legend which is at the bottom of Wagner's drama is formed of two portions which were once distinct. One of these portions is concerned with the origin and wanderings of the Holy Grail prior to the time when it became the object of the Quest which occupied so much of the attention of the knights of King Arthur's Round Table; the second portion is concerned with that Quest. The relative age of the two portions of the legend and the genesis of each have caused much controversy, which has thrown a great deal of light on mediæval civilization. We are little concerned in that controversy, however, except so far as it enlightens us as to the real nature of the legend, and helps us to understand how the Grail became the loftiest symbol of Christian faith, and the Grail Quest the highest duty of Christian knighthood.

Formerly it was believed that the Grail was the product of Christian legends which had become grafted on the Arthurian romances. Now it is asserted, and with much show of probability, that the Grail, like those romances, is Celtic in origin, and became what it is represented in the legend by being endowed with a symbolism which originally it lacked. For our view of the case, since we are not concerned with literary criticism, this, too, is a matter of indifference, except so far as it helps us to understand a proposition much broader and more significant. The Holy Grail and the Seeker after it are both relics of what, long before Christianity was in existence, was a universal possession among Aryan peoples. Each has a multitude of prototypes among the mythological apparatus and personages of the peoples of the Indo-European family. To the class of popular heroes which figure in the tales whose essential elements Von Hahn has formulated in his *Arische Aussetzung und Rückkehr Formel* (see Chapter IV.), Parsifal belongs as well as Siegfried. A parallel between the two might be carried through many details of their early life and riper adventures. Both are born to a mother, far from her home, of a father who is dead; both are brought up in a wilderness; both are in youth passionate and violent of disposition; both are thrown for companionship on the animals of the forests in which they are reared. There are other elements held in common by the tales of which Wagner makes no mention in his version of the Percival legend. A significant one is the mending of a broken sword, a talisman, which act in the old Percival legends, as well as in the tale of Siegfried, is the sign of the hero's election to a high mission; but this need not now detain us.

Wagner has been much criticized for changing the name of his hero from Percival or Percivale, as we know it in English literature, and Parzival, as he found it in the greatest of all the Grail epics, that of Wolfram von Eschenbach, to Parsifal. Criticism of this kind is often wasted. In making the change Wagner exercised a poet's privilege for an obvious purpose—he made the name an index of his hero's moral character. The suggestion came from Görres. According to this scholar, whose derivation has long been set aside as fanciful, *Fal* in the Arabian tongue signifies "foolish," and *Parsi* "pure one." By changing the order of the words we obtain Parsi-fal—pure, or guileless, fool. It is thus that Kundry expounds his name to the hero in Wagner's drama, when she tells him the story of his birth. In Wolfram's poem he is also called foolish because his mother dressed him in motley when he left her, broken-hearted, to go out into the world in search of knighthood. The French Perceval signifies simply one who goes "through the Valley." A Welsh tale of at least equal antiquity with the preserved French romances calls the hero Peredur, which has been interpreted into "the seeker after the basin or the dish," this signification being again in harmony with the principal incident of the French form of the legend, *greal* in old French meaning a dish. Wolfram, under the influence of his model, claims nothing for the name of his hero except that it means "right through the middle," but Meyer-Markau, who seems to have accepted the theory that the tale is originally Keltic, strove to give dramatic propriety to the name by pointing out that in Welsh, Breton, and Cornish, *par* signifies lad; *syw*, in Welsh, clad or decorated, and *fall*, scantily, poorly, ill, foolishly, wretchedly. Out of these words, then, he compounded *Par-syw-fall*, a lad who is ill-clad. Plausibility, if nothing else, is lent to this derivation by the circumstances under which the hero's mother sent him out into the world. In the hope that the rude treatment which would be heaped upon him would return him to her arms, she dressed him in fool's clothing:

"'Thorenkleider soll mein Kind
An seinem lichten Leibe tragen:
Schlägt und rauft man ihn darum,
So kommt er mir wohl wieder.'
Weh, was litt die Arme da!
Nun nahm sie grobes Sacktuch her
Und schnitt ihm Hemd und Hose draus
In einem Stück, das bis zum Knie
Des nackten Beins nur reichte.
Das war als Narrenkleid bekannt.
Oben sah man eine Kappe." [1]

III.

Interesting as this speculation is, however, we are now concerned only with one element of it. Whatever his name may signify, it is obvious that Parsifal was an innocent, a *simplex*, a fool. It is this trait which enables us to identify him with his prototype in Aryan folk-lore. He is the hero of what the English folk-lorists call "The Great Fool Tales," and the Germans "*Dümmlingsmärchen*." In the following outline of a very old poetic narrative of the Kelts, called by students "The Lay of the Great Fool," may be found all that part of Parsifal's youthful history which, in Wagner's drama, is learned either from his own lips or those of Kundry:

Once there were two knightly brothers, of whom one was childless while the other had two sons. A strife breaks out between them, and the father is slain with his sons. The wicked knight then sends word to the widow that if she should give birth to another son, he, too, must be put to death. She does give birth to a son, and to save his life sends him into the wilderness to be reared by a kitchen wench who has a love-son. The lads grow up strong and hardy. One day the knightly lad runs down a deer, kills it, and of its skin makes himself a motley suit of clothes. He slays his foster-brother for laughing at him in his strange dress, catches a wild horse, rides to his uncle's palace, and though when asked his name he can only answer "Great Fool," he is recognized. Thus his adventures begin. He avenges the wrongs of his mother. This Great Fool is the original Seeker after the Grail.

IV.

Among the oldest manuscripts which contain the Quest story there are two which make no mention of the Holy Grail as a Christian relic or symbol. The most interesting of these is Welsh, and is known as the Mabinogi (*i. e.*, the Juvenile Tale) of "Peredur, the Son of Evrawc." It is an Arthurian story, and the majority of its adventures are identical with those of Percival. Its beginning is a parallel of "The Lay of the Great Fool." The Holy Grail of the Percival romances is replaced by a bleeding lance, a bloody head on a salver, and a silver dish. These talismans are brought into the hall of a castle belonging to a lame king, and are greeted with loud lamentations by the assembled knights. In the French romances the talismans are the Holy Grail and the bleeding lance, the latter being identified, as in Sir Thomas Malory's "Morte d'Arthur," with the spear with which Longinus opened the side of the crucified Christ. As Percival is condemned in these romances for a long time to wander in fruitless search of this castle, because having seen the wonders he did not ask their meaning, so Peredur, in the Welsh romance, is cursed in the Court of King Arthur for a similar neglect. Had he asked, the lame king would have got well of his wound, and Peredur would have proved his fitness to avenge the death of his cousin, who was the lame king's son, and had been killed by the sorceresses of Gloucester. After many trials, tallying with those of Percival in the French romances and Parzival in Wolfram's poem, Peredur finds the castle again (where he had on his first visit united the pieces of a broken sword and cut through an iron staple, as Siegfried split the anvil), is recognized as the nephew of the king, and avenges his cousin's death by leading Arthur and his knights against the sorceresses of Gloucester. There are some allusions to the Christian religion in the old tale, but essentially it is pagan. The bloody head and bleeding lance are part of ancient British legendary apparatus.

A bleeding lance, says Mr. Alfred Nutt,[K] is the bardic symbol of undying hatred of the Saxon. Here it bled till the death of Peredur's cousin was avenged. The bloody head was the head of that cousin.

V.

We find in Parsifal on his entrance only a thoughtless, impetuous forest lad, unlearned in the affairs of life, utterly unconscious of its conventions—in short, another young Siegfried. He is the hero of the "Great Fool" stories, but in the process of Christianizing the character a new meaning has been given to the epithet. He is a chosen vessel for a divine deed, because he is a pure or guileless fool. In this, though the suggestion was derived from the old Aryan folk-tales, we are obliged to see a new, a Christian symbolism, the spirit of which may be found in Christ's words, "Whosoever shall not receive the kingdom of God as a *little child* shall not enter it." In Wagner's conception of the legend it was necessary that the hero be one as guiltless of all knowledge of sin as he was of the necessity and nature of salvation. Enlightenment was to come to him through compassion or fellow-suffering, and this enlightenment was to enable him in turn to resist temptation and bring surcease of suffering to Amfortas, Kundry, and the community of Grail knights. In his musical phrase as it enters the drama with him one may hear chiefly his youthful energy, but also a certain innate dignity, a germ of nobility which contains the possibility of the stupendous proclamation which greets him on his entrance into the Castle of the Grail in the last act. But there is another element in the typical music of "Parsifal" which chiefly we recognize in its bright, assertive, militant rhythm. It is the chivalric element which may also be noticed in the brilliant phrase with which Lohengrin, the son of Parsifal, is greeted by the populace in the earlier drama of Wagner's. This kinship need not be set down as fanciful. There are few features of Wagnerian study more interesting than the tracing of spiritual and material parallels between the composer's own melodies. As a writer uses forms of expression which resemble each other to express related ideas, so Wagner has frequently recurred in his later works to melodic phrases and modulations which he had used with like intent many years before. In two cases he made a direct quotation. Hans Sachs's allusion to the story of Tristram and Iseult in Act III. of "Die Meistersinger" is accompanied by the fundamental melody of "Tristan und Isolde," and the swan which Parsifal kills comes fluttering across the scene and dies to a reminiscence of the swan harmonies in "Lohengrin."

In his character as the mystically chosen Agent of the Grail and the instrument of salvation, Parsifal is also typified in the music by the phrase to which the oracular promise which appeared on the Holy Vessel is repeated in the first scene, and again with great solemnity in the ceremony of the Adoration of the Grail.

VI.

Prototypes of the Quest of the Grail and of the Quester have been found in popular tales which have nothing to do with Christianity. Until the talisman became a symbol of religion, the object of the search for it was simply the performance of a sacred duty by the hero to his family, by avenging a death, healing the lingering illness of a relative, or in some instances (which connect the Grail legends with stories of the Barbarossa kind) to bring freedom to individuals whose lives have been miraculously and burdensomely prolonged. The talisman itself is to be found in a multitude of forms, from the dawn of literature down to today. To recognize it we must study its properties rather than its shape or material. In the legend of the Holy Grail it is the chalice used by Christ

"At the last sad supper with his own,"

in which afterwards his blood was caught. In one form of the legend—that which is most familiar, because of Tennyson's "Idyls of the King"—this cup is carried to Great Britain by Joseph of Arimathea and deposited at Glastonbury. In another form, which was that adopted by Wagner, it is given into the keeping of Titurel, who builds a sanctuary for it on Monsalvat (the Mountain of Salvation), where it is guarded by a body of knights obviously organized on the model of the Knights Templars of the Crusades. It is not always a cup. Wolfram von Eschenbach describes it as a jewel. But whether stone or cup (and we shall find prototypes of both forms) its miraculous properties are of two kinds.

The first of these properties is purely physical: the talisman feeds its possessor; the second is spiritual: the talisman is a touchstone, an oracle. In the perfect form of the legend both these properties are united, as we see in Wagner's drama: the Grail chooses those who are to serve it, and nourishes them miraculously. It also predicts the coming of Parsifal. This is the case, too, in Wolfram's poem, where the names of the elect appear in glowing letters upon the jewel, and its guardian knights, whom Wolfram calls *Templeisen*, are fed by it, this miraculous power being refreshed every Friday by the coming of a dove bringing the sacred host and placing it upon the jewel, which Wolfram calls the "Graal," in defiance of the etymology which makes the word mean dish. Wolfram calls it "*lapsit exillis*;" but Wolfram, though he composed the grandest of all mediæval poems, could neither read nor write, so his Latin has caused not a little brain-cudgelling among the learned. A most ingenious guess is that of Professor Martin, who thinks *lapsit exillis* is a corruption of *lapsi de Cælis*—that is, the stone of him who fell from heaven. In support of this there is the poem about the contest of the minstrels in the Wartburg, which describes the Grail as a jewel which fell from the crown of Lucifer when the Archangel Michael tore it from his head. This origin of the Grail connects it with the black stone in the Kaaba at Mecca, which was originally white, but has been blackened by the sins of mankind. The legend says that it was once the angel set as a guard over Adam. He was cast down from heaven in the form of a stone for being derelict in duty.

The Grail's property of furnishing sustenance is the possession of so many talismans of ancient story that it would be a waste of space to enumerate them all. The most striking examples must suffice. A horn was the earliest drinking-vessel. The horn which the nymph Amalthea gave to Hercules, whose memory we still preserve in those pretty toys called cornucopias—horns of plenty—is easily recalled in this connection. The Grail is nothing else than the Philosopher's Stone which was to transmute all baser metals into gold; it is the stone which Noah was commanded to hang up in the Ark that it might give out light; it is the goblet which Oberon gave to Huon of Bordeaux, which in the hands of a good man became filled with wine; it is the golden cup which was given to Hercules by the sun-god Helios; it is the cup of Hermes, which played a part in the Eleusinian mysteries; it is the magic napkin or table-cloth of Aryan fairy-lore which produced all manner of food simply for the wishing; it has its fellows in three of the thirteen Rarities of Kingly Regalia which were preserved in Arthur's Court at Caerleon, viz., the horn of Bran the Hardy of the North—the drink that might be desired of it would appear as soon as wished for; the Budget or Basket of Gwyddno with the High Crown—provision for a single person if put into it multiplied a hundredfold; the table-cloth (in one manuscript it is called the dish) of Rhydderch the Scholar—whatever victuals or drink were wished thereon were instantly obtained. It is the stone in the serpent's tail told about in the old Welsh story of Peredur, the virtue of which was that it would give as much gold to the possessor as he might desire. It is the magic ring Draupnir of Scandinavian mythology which every ninth night dropped eight other rings of equal weight and fineness.

But of prototypes of this class the most striking in its relation to the Holy Grail is found in the legendary lore of the primitive home of the Aryan race. Long ago the Holy Grail was the Golden Cup of Jamshid, King of the Genii in Persia, the power of which extended his career over seven hundred years, and then left him to die because he failed to look upon it for ten days. Here we have a parallel of the legend of Joseph of Arimathea, of whom it is said that the Jews having thrown him into a subterranean prison after he and Nicodemus had prepared the body of Christ for burial, Christ appeared to him and brought the chalice which he had used at the Last Supper, and in which Joseph had caught the blood which flowed from his wounds. The sight of this dish kept Joseph alive forty-two years, until he was released by the Emperor Vespasian, who had been miraculously cured of leprosy in his youth by a touch of the kerchief of Veronica with which Christ wiped his face while on his way to Calvary. Like Joseph of Arimathea, Wagner's Titurel lives in his grave, being sustained by the Grail until Amfortas refuses longer to unveil it.

The second property of the Grail, its spiritual property, is also found in the talismans of ancient folk-lore. It was possessed by the silver cup which Joseph in Egypt had put into Benjamin's sack that he might be brought back to him. "Up, follow after the men; and when thou dost overtake them, say unto them, Wherefore have ye rewarded evil for good? Is not this it in which my lord drinketh and whereby, indeed, he divineth?"[L] There is a Hebrew legend (told in the *Clavicula Salomonis*) to the effect that "the supernatural knowledge of Solomon was recorded in a volume which Rehoboam inclosed in an ivory ewer and deposited in his father's tomb. On repairing the sepulchre, some wise men of Babylon discovered the cup, and having extracted the volume, an angel revealed the key to its mysterious writing to one Troes, a Greek, and hence the stream of occult science which has so beneficially unfolded the destinies of the West."[M] There is a parallel story in Greek literature telling how, warned by the Delphic oracle,

Aristomenes secreted an article while the Lacedemonians were storming the fortress of Mount Ira. The article was to be a talisman for the future security of the Messinians. When, later, the talisman was exhumed it was "found to be a brazen ewer containing a roll of finely-beaten tin on which were inscribed the mysteries of the great divinities."[N] The Holy Grail is a divining-cup: it speaks oracularly, like its prototypes. It was not only the chalice from which Christ drank at the Last Supper, but also the dish which discovered Judas as the future betrayer of his master: "He that dippeth his hand with me in the dish, the same shall betray me."[O]

VII.

The Grail romances, as we possess them, were written within the fifty years compassing the last quarter of the twelfth and the first quarter of the thirteenth centuries—that is to say, while the third and fourth crusades were in progress, and the memory of the supposed discoveries of the sacred cup and lance were still fresh in the minds of Europeans. This fact furnishes ample suggestion as to how such talismans as I have mentioned became transformed into the relics of Christ's passion. It was by a literary process that has always been familiar to the world. The species of belief or superstition which inspired the transformation is not yet dead. If we are to believe Father Ignatius the miracle of the Grail vision was repeated but recently at Llanthony Abbey in Wales, where an Episcopal monk saw the chalice shining through the oaken doors of the cabinet which enclosed it. That is a Christian form of the belief; evidences of a pagan may be observed in nearly all civilized communities almost any date. When you see a baby cutting its teeth upon a red bit of bone, or ivory shaped like a branch of coral and tricked out with bells, you see a relic of an unspeakably ancient superstition closely allied to the belief in these miraculous talismans. When you see a baby with a string of red coral beads around its neck you see another. In Wagner, as in Tennyson, the Grail shines red:

"Fainter by day, but always in the night
Blood-red, and sliding down the blacken'd marsh
Blood-red, and on the naked mountain-top
Blood-red, and in the sleeping mere below
Blood-red."

Now note this truth of vast significance: the essential element in the Grail, whether seen as a chalice or as a salver containing a head, *is the blood*. The meaning of this need not be sought far. The human imagination cannot be projected into the past sufficiently far to picture the time when the awful idea of a bloody atonement did not confront humanity. Hence it is that in pagan mythology blood is the symbol of creative power, as the cups, horns, dishes, ewers, were symbols of fecundity, abundance, and vivification. The essence of the Grail myth is the reproductive power of the blood of a slain god. The application which lies so near in a study of the Christian symbolism of the Grail cannot fail. I omit it in order to trace the evolution of the idea in a pagan talisman whose history the ingenuity of Dr. Gustave Oppert, a German *savant*, has disclosed to us. When Perseus cut off the head of the Medusa he placed the bleeding member on the sward near the sea-coast. The blood transformed the grass that it dyed into a red stone which was found to have marvellous healing power. This belief is expressed in the poems descriptive of the virtues of stones which are attributed to Orpheus. Dr. Oppert traces the record touching the curative powers of coral into the book of a Christian bishop of the twelfth century, and thence into a Latin work printed in Strassburg in 1473, in which allusions to the Orphic songs and the Christian religion are blended. Wolfram's alleged model, Kyot, professes to have derived his account of the Grail from the book of a pagan called Flegetanis, written in Arabic and deposited at Toledo. Now, Dr. Oppert finds an Arabic physician and philosopher of the tenth century who describes coral as having a strengthening and nourishing influence upon the heart, which belief seems recognized again in a bit of mediæval etymology which compounds the word of *cor* and *alere*. Mediæval Latin poems express the belief that peculiar properties of sustenance are possessed by coral, and, finally, in a book entitled *Musæum Metallicum* it is defined as a memorial of the blood of Christ. In its physical attributes coral and the Grail are now identical. Had Dr. Oppert wished, he might have gone further and quoted Pliny's remark that the Indian soothsayers and diviners "look upon coral as an amulet endowed with sacred properties and a sure preservative against all dangers; hence it is that they equally value it as an ornament and as an object of devotion."[P] Here spiritual properties are attributed to it; but also physical. Pliny says that calcined coral is used as an ingredient for compositions for the eyes; that it makes flesh (very significant this) in cavities left by ulcers. In his day it was hung about the necks of infants to preserve them against danger. The Romans thought that it preserved and fastened the teeth of children when hung about their necks. Paracelsus prescribed coral necklaces as preservatives "against fits, sorcery, charms, and poison," and an old English writer makes it disclose the presence of sickness in a wearer by turning pale and wan. Here it is a touchstone, and this superstition has penetrated to the United States. In our day I have been told by devoted mothers that coral beads strengthen the eyes. When the present Crown-prince of Italy was born in Naples the municipality presented the royal babe with a coral cradle.

Thus much for the genesis of the Grail, its Quest, and its Quester. We have seen that they are all relics of a time antedating Christianity; but that fact only adds interest to them, for even in their pagan guises they show those potential attributes which adapted them to receive the lofty symbolism which they acquired under the influence of Christianity.

VIII.

It is in the prelude to the drama that the fundamental elements of suffering and aspiration are most eloquently proclaimed. The visible symbol of suffering among the personages of the play is Amfortas. He, too, has come into the Christianized legend from the secular romances and folk-tales. In the earlier forms he is simply the representative of unsatisfied vengeance, symbolized in the bardic emblem of the bleeding lance. In the French romances and Wolfram's poem he is a royal fisherman—a singular fact, which critics with a taste for hidden meanings have sought to explain by references to the circumstance that in the early Church a fish was a symbol for Christ, the letters composing its name in Greek, ICHTHYS, being the initial letters of the brief but comprehensive creed, *Iesous Christos, Theou Yios, Soter* (Jesus Christ, God's Son, Saviour). But always, even in the Welsh tale, he is a sufferer whose healing depends on the asking of a question by a predestined hero. In the Mabinogi of Peredur and the French romances the question goes simply to the meaning of the talismans which are solemnly displayed. Wolfram deepens the ethical significance of the question immeasurably by changing it to "What ails thee, uncle?" It is the sympathy thus manifested that brings the fisher-king's sufferings to an end; and the failure to ask the question on the first visit, through a too literal interpretation of the advice given while Parzival was receiving his education in chivalry, is the cause of the long wanderings and many trials which test and temper the religious nature of Parzival. Wagner, by ignoring the question which plays so important a role in all the other versions, and making the healing of Amfortas depend upon a touch of the sacred lance, has gained a theatrical effect at the expense of a profoundly beautiful ethical principle. He has also laid himself open to a charge of inconsistency which, strangely enough, seems to have escaped the attention of his many inimical critics in Germany. The prohibited question is the dramatic *motif* upon which the story of Percival's son, Lohengrin, is reared:

"Nie sollst du mich befragen,
Noch Wissens Sorge tragen,
Woher ich kam der Fahrt,
Noch wie mein Nam' und Art!"

The reason of the prohibition may be learned from Wolfram von Eschenbach. The sufferings of Amfortas having been needlessly prolonged by Parzival's failure to ask the healing question, the Knights of the Grail thereafter refused to permit themselves to be questioned:

"Als die Taufe nun geschen,
Fand am Grale man geschrieben:
'Welchen Templer Gottes Hand
Fremdem Volk zum Herren gäbe,
Fragen sollt' er widerraten
Nach seinem Namen und Geschlecht,
Und dann zum Recht ihm helfen.
Wird die Frage doch gethan,
So bleibt er ihnen länger nicht.'
Weil der gute Amfortas
So lang im bittern Schemerzen lag,
Und ihn die Frage lange mied,
Ist ihnen alles Fragen leid:
All des Grales Dienstgesellen
Wolln sich nicht mehr fragen lassen."[Q]

Wagner utilized the *motif* in "Lohengrin," but ignored it in "Parsifal."

The suffering of Amfortas, which came upon him because he, the King of the Grail, fell from the estate of bodily purity enjoined by the rules of the order, receives more eloquent expression than any of the other feelings which enter the drama. In Wagner's philosophical scheme it, as well as the tortures of conscience felt by Parsifal when Kundry's impure kiss awakens him to consciousness of transgression, recalls the vicarious suffering of Christ on the Cross. In the personal history of Parsifal, furthermore, it is associated with the death-agonies of his mother, who died because he left her to go in search of knighthood. The name of this mother Wagner changes so that it becomes a symbol of pain. It is Herzeleide—that is, Heart's-sorrow, or Heart's-suffering, the antithesis of our sweet English word Heart's-ease. The phrases which give the predominant mood of agony and pain to the music of the drama, which, as I have already said, reflect the spirit of theological Christianity, salvation through sacrifice, are these:

First. The melody to which in the ceremony of the Adoration of the Grail the sacramental formula is pronounced: "Take ye My Body, take My Blood, in token of our Love."

Second. The personal melody of Amfortas.

Third. The symbol of Herzeleide. Parsifal's mother, does not enter the drama, but is only spoken of; yet a typical phrase is allotted to her, and is introduced for the first time under circumstances that are profoundly poetical and pathetic. Parsifal is being questioned by Gurnemanz. To all interrogations save one he has the single answer, "I do not know." Asked his name, he answers: "Once I had many, but now I remember none." This answer is accompanied by the Herzeleide phrase. To find the clue to this somewhat enigmatic proceeding resort must be had to Wagner's model Wolfram, where it is said of the lad's mother that

"A thousand times she said tenderly:
'Bon fils, cher fils, beau fils.'"

These were the names which Parsifal once knew but had forgotten. They are associated in his mind with his mother, and therefore the allusion is accompanied by the Herzeleide phrase.

Fourth. The phrase to which in the memorial ceremony of Christ's suffering the words are sung:

"For a world that slumbered
With sorrows unnumbered
He once His own blood offered."

It is this phrase that lends such great poignancy to the music which accompanies Parsifal and Gurnemanz as they walk towards the Castle of the Grail.

In the prelude suffering has its expression in the first of these phrases, whose concluding figure in the second part reaches an expression of agony like the cry that rent the air of Calvary even as the curtain of the temple was rent in twain: "*Eli, Eli, lama sabachthani?*" Aspiration is proclaimed by the symbol of the Grail itself, the familiar Amen formula of the Dresden Court Church, an ethereal phrase which soars ever upward towards the zenith of tonality. The melody of Faith is marked by lofty firmness, and derives a peculiar emphasis from successive repetition in remote keys.

For the prelude, whose melodic material has been thus marshalled, we have Wagner's own poetic exposition:

"Strong and firm does Faith reveal itself, elevated and resolute even in suffering. In answer to the renewed promise the voice of Faith sounds softly from dimmest heights—as though borne on the wings of the snow-white dove—slowly descending, embracing with ever-increasing breadth and fulness the heart of man, filling the world and the whole of nature with mightiest force; then, as though stilled to rest, glancing upward again towards the light of heaven. Then once more from the awe of solitude arises the lament of loving compassion, the agony, the holy sweat of the

Mount of Olives, the divine sufferings of Golgotha; the body blanches, the blood streams forth and glows now with the 'heavenly glow of blessing in the chalice, pouring forth on all that lives and languishes the gracious gift of Redemption through Love. For him we are prepared, for Amfortas, the sinful guardian of the shrine who, with fearful rue for sin gnawing at his heart, must prostrate himself before the chastisement of the vision of the Grail. Shall there be redemption from the devouring torments of his soul? Yet once again we hear the promise and—hope!"

IX.

The first act of the drama treats of the election of the hero, the guileless simpleton of the talismanic oracle. In the second stage of the action the hero is proved by temptation. All the elements here are derived from legendary stories, but in their combination Wagner has proceeded with remarkable dramatic power, freedom, and ingenuity. The apparatus is magical. Klingsor, a pervasive personage in mediæval sorcery; Kundry, the repulsive messenger of the Grail no longer, but a supernaturally beautiful siren; a magic garden and castle, and a bevy of maidens, whose office it is to stimulate the senses by suggesting an appeal to all of them at once (they are half human, half floral)—these are the agencies of Parsifal's temptation. The prototype of the scene in old mythologies and folk-lore is a visit to a bespelled castle where generally the hero succumbs to sensual weakness of some kind; he eats of proffered food and loses his speech; or he asks a question which is *tabu*; or he fails to ask a question which is commanded; or falls asleep; or fails to bring away a talisman which has opened the castle to him; or he falls as Tannhäuser fell. As a rule the castle vanishes at the end of the adventure, as it does in "Parsifal," when the hero resists Kundry's love-spell, seizes the lance which the magician launches against him, and with it makes the sign of the cross and pronounces a formula of exorcism. Often the purpose of the visit is to release a damsel who is bespelled or imprisoned. Students of comparative folk-lore have found the mythological essence of the stories of this class to lie in a visit to the underworld. Siegfried achieved an analogous adventure when he penetrated the wall of fire, and awakened Brünnhilde from the spell of sleep in which she was held.

Klingsor is remotely connected with the history of two other dramas of Wagner. In the poem describing the Contest of Minstrelsy held in the Wartburg which Wagner blended with the legend of Tannhäuser, Klingsor is a magician and minstrel of Hungary, and to him Heinrich von Effterdingen, otherwise Tannhäuser, appeals when defeated by Wolfram von Eschenbach, who is not only the author of the poem "Parzival," but also the tuneful minstrel who sings a woful ballad to the evening star in

Wagner's opera. In his epic Wolfram makes Klingsor a nephew of the renowned magician Virgilius of Naples.[R]

Cyriacus Spangenberg, who wrote a book on the Art of the Master-singers in 1598, devotes several pages to Klingsor, describing him as the greatest master-singer of his age, who met all comers in poetical combat and overthrew them to the number of fifty-two. He was finally confounded by Wolfram von Eschenbach, who discovered his dependence on the Powers of Evil, and put both him and his familiar, a devil called Nazian, to shame by singing the glories of the Son of God become Man.

"Kundry," says Mr. Alfred Nutt, "is Wagner's greatest contribution to the legend. She is the Herodias whom Christ, for her laughter, doomed to wander till He come again." The manner in which Wagner compounded this, his most striking and original dramatic character, is the most marvellous of his poetical achievements in the drama. Kundry draws her elements from the Grail romances, from Christian legends, from fairy tales, and from the profoundest depths of the poet's imagination. In the Welsh tale her prototype is the hero's cousin, who is under a spell, and in accordance with the popular tale formula appears as a loathly damsel until her kinsman achieves the vengeance demanded by family ties. Then she appears in her true form as a handsome youth. In Wolfram, Kundrie la Sorcière is only the Grail Messenger, and as such is hideous of appearance; the temptress of the Magic Garden is a beauteous damsel named Orgeluse. Wagner united both attributes in his creation. As a penitent, seeking atonement for sin committed, she is a loathly damsel in the service of the Grail. As a siren she is a tool of Klingsor, to whose power she is subject while asleep. She has innumerable prototypes in fairy-lore, who are released from wicked spells by the kisses of handsome princes, the fidelity of husbands, or the granting of their wills, as in "The Marriage of Sir Gawaine." In Wagner, the dissolution of the spell releases her from a double curse. The suggestion to make use of the Herodias legend lies near enough in both the Mabinogi of Peredur and Wolfram's epic. The Templeisen, as Wolfram calls his Knights of the Grail, were an order obviously patterned after the Knights Templars, who were accused among other things of having secretly worshipped a head which they credited with the virtues of the talismans that I have discussed. Their patron saint was John the Baptist, and when the vessel of green glass, so long and piously revered as the *santo catino*, was brought back by crusaders seven hundred years ago, it was deposited in the Chapel of St. John at Genoa. A relic of the John the Baptist cult has survived among the Knights Templar, a branch of the Order of Free Masons, to this day. That the talisman of a bloody head upon a salver in the Welsh tale should have suggested the Herodias legend is obvious enough. Wagner's transformation of the legend, accomplished for the purpose of identifying his Kundry with Herodias, is extremely suggestive and felicitous. According to the old tale, Herodias was in love with the prophet of the New Dispensation. After the dance before Herod and its awful consequences, she secretly crept to the head upon the salver for the purpose of covering it with tears and kisses. At that moment a blast issued from the dead lips which sent Herodias flying off into space. Thus she is still driven forward, permitted to rest only from midnight to dawn, when she sits cowering under willow and hazel copses, and bemoans her fate. In Wagner she becomes a Wandering Jewess. She saw Christ staggering under the burden of the Cross and laughed. His glance fell upon her, and doomed her to wander ceaselessly without the sweet refuge of tears, subject to the powers of evil, yet longing to make atonement by deeds of virtue. These characteristics Wagner developed with marvellous dramatic power in the music which he associates with her, and which is equally wild and hysterical, whether it picture her flying along on a horse doing errands in the service of the Grail, or in one of those fits of mad laughter to which the curse makes her subject.

Yet Kundry, to proceed with Mr. Nutt, "would find release and salvation could a man resist her love spell. She knows this. The scene between the unwilling temptress, whose success would but doom her afresh, and the virgin Parsifal thus becomes tragic in the extreme. How does this affect Amfortas and the Grail? In this way: Parsifal is the pure fool, knowing naught of sin or suffering. It had been foretold of him that he should become 'wise by fellow-suffering,' and so it proves. The overmastering rush of desire unseals his eyes, clears his mind. Heart-wounded by the shaft of passion, he feels Amfortas' torture thrill through him. The pain of the physical wound is his, but far more, the agony of the sinner who has been unworthy of his high trust, and who, soiled by carnal sin, must yet daily come in contact with the Grail, symbol of the highest purity and holiness. The strength of the new-born knowledge enables him to resist sensual longing, and thereby to release both Kundry and Amfortas."

X.

In spite of this, however, and more than this, in spite of all the religious mysticism with which the work can be infused by the analyst and interpreter, I cannot but question the right of "Parsifal" to be considered as in any sense a reflex of the religious feeling of to-day. It is beautiful in much of its symbolism, and it is profound; but it is too persistently mediæval in its dramatic manifestations to satisfy the intelligence of the nineteenth century. The adoration of the relics of Christ's passion, and the idea that all human virtues are summed up in celibate chastity, were products of an age whose theories and practices as regards sex relationship can have no echo in modern civilization. Wolfram von Eschenbach's married Parzival, who clings with fond devotion to the memory of the wife from whose arms he had to tear himself in order to undertake the quest, and who loses himself in tender brooding for a long time when the sight of blood-spots on the snow suggests to his fancy the red and white of his wife's cheeks, seems to me to be a much more amiable and human hero than the young ascetic of Wagner's drama.

FOOTNOTES:

[J] *Parzival, von Wolfram von Eschenbach.* Dr. Gotthold Bötticher. Berlin, 1885.

[K] *Studies on the Legend of the Holy Grail.* David Nutt. London, 1888.

[L] Genesis xliv., 4 and 5.

[M] Mr. Price's Preface in Warton's *History of English Poetry*, vol. i.

[N] Mr. Price's note in Warton, vol. i.

[O] Matthew xxvi., 23.

[P] Natural History, Book XXXII., chap. ii.

[Q] Bötticher's Translation Book XVI.

[R] The stories concerning Virgil and his connection with the Black Art are admirably discussed in Mr. J. S. Tunison's study, *Master Virgil, the Author of the Æneid as he seemed in the Middle Ages*. Second Edition. Robert Clarke & Co. Cincinnati, 1890.